Basketball's
Most Wanted™ II

To ~~John~~
~~Sergentberles~~ ;

my mentor, hero,
boss — and
friend !

Merry Xmas
+
Happy New
Year !
— David L. Hurds,
Jr.

Also by David L. Hudson, Jr.

Boxing's Most Wanted™: The Top 10 Book of Champs, Chumps, and Punch-Drunk Palookas (with Mike Fitzgerald, Jr.)

The Fourteenth Amendment: Equal Protection Under the Law

The Bill of Rights: The First Ten Amendments of the Constitution

Basketball's Most Wanted™ II

The Top 10 Book of More Hotshot
Hoopsters, Double Dribbles, and
Roundball Oddities

David L. Hudson, Jr.

Potomac Books, Inc.
Washington, D.C.

Copyright © 2005 by Potomac Books, Inc.

Published in the United States by Potomac Books, Inc.
All rights reserved. No part of this book may be
reproduced in any manner whatsoever without
written permission from the publisher, except in the
case of brief quotations embodied in critical
articles and reviews.

Library of Congress Cataloging-in-Publication Data

Hudson, David L., 1969–
    Basketball's most wanted II : the top 10 book
of more hotshot hoopsters, double dribbles, and
roundball oddities / David L. Hudson, Jr.—1st ed.
        p.   cm.—(Most wanted)
    Includes bibliographical references and index.
    ISBN 1-57488-950-8 (pbk. : alk. paper)
    1. Basketball—Miscellanea.   I. Title:
Basketball's most wanted 2.   II. Title: Basketball's
most wanted two.   III. Title.   IV. Series.
GV885.H79   2005
796.357—dc22   2005007482

Printed in Canada on acid-free paper that meets
the American National Standards Institute
Z39–48 Standard.

Potomac Books, Inc.
22841 Quicksilver Drive
Dulles, Virginia 20166

First Edition

10   9   8   7   6   5   4   3   2   1

*To Bill Clark—a former basketball star,
the best free throw shooter I've ever encountered,
a mentor and a great friend.*

Contents

Photographs

Acknowledgments

The author wishes to thank the following people: John Heacock, Bill Clark, Jay Jackson, Mike Williamson, Marshall Terrill, Chris Collins, Sean Stormes, Sean Foley, Brad Emerson, Greg Korn, and, most of all, my sportswriting mentor Mike Fitzgerald.

National Championship Game Performances

The crown jewel of college basketball remains the Final Four, where four teams battle it out for National Collegiate Athletic Association (NCAA) supremacy in the season-ending tournament. Several players have starred on March Madness's biggest stage. These players saved their best for the NCAA championship game.

1. **BILL WALTON**

Bill Walton, "the Big Redhead," dominated college basketball during his days at UCLA, proving to be a worthy successor to Lew Alcindor (later Kareem Abdul-Jabbar). In 1973, Walton led the Bruins to a win over Indiana in the semifinals and a convincing 87–66 thumping of Memphis State in the finals. In the championship game, Walton scored 44 points, hitting 21 out of 22 shots. Walton grabbed 13 rebounds in the title game en route to earning Most Outstanding Player (MOP) honors. Many consider Walton's title–game performance as the greatest single game effort by a college basketball player.

2. **PERVIS ELLISON**

The 1986 title game featured the high-flying Louisville Cardinals against the best team in college basketball that year, the Duke Blue Devils. Duke—led by senior stars Johnny Dawkins, Mark Alarie, David Henderson, and Jay Bilas—lost only one game the entire regular season. However, in the title game Duke had no answer for Louisville freshman center Pervis "Never Nervous" Ellison. Ellison scored 24 points on 10 for 14 shooting, and also grabbed 11 rebounds. Ellison became only the second freshman to earn the tournament's MOP award.

3. **JACK GIVENS**

In 1978, Kentucky battled Duke for the national championship. Kentucky had an outstanding guard in Kyle Macy, their floor leader, and a bruising big man in Rick Robey. But the star of the show was their smooth-shooting forward Jack "Goose" Givens, who never played better than in the 1978 title game. He scored 41 points, shooting 18 for 27 from the field.

4. **GAIL GOODRICH**

In the 1965 title game, UCLA captured its second straight national championship with a 91–80 victory over the University of Michigan. In the battle of shooters, UCLA's Gail Goodrich outgunned Michigan star Cazzie Russell 42–28. Goodrich shot 12 for 22 from the field and an amazing 18 out of 20 from the free throw line for his impressive final game performance. Amazingly, Goodrich's final game performance failed to earn him the tournament's MOP award. That's because Princeton's Bill Bradley scored 87 points during the Final Four, including 58 points in a single game.

5. GLEN RICE

No one could have predicted that Michigan would win the 1989 NCAA tournament. Just prior to the tournament their coach, Bill Frieder, was replaced after he revealed he was taking the head job at Arizona State. Assistant coach Steve Fisher was installed as interim coach and the Wolverines rolled to the title, including a thrilling 80–79 overtime win over Seton Hall. The Wolverines won largely because of sharp-shooting star forward Glen Rice. In the final game Rice connected for 31 points, including five three-pointers. During the six games he scored a record 184 points. The record still stands as the most points by an individual in a single NCAA tournament.

6. LEW ALCINDOR

Lew Alcindor may have been the most dominant force in the history of college basketball. He was college basketball's Most Valuable Player (MVP) all three years of his college career (freshman were not eligible in Alcindor's day), and UCLA captured national titles in all three of those years. In 1969, Alcindor led the Bruins to a 92–72 destruction of Purdue. The hapless Boilermakers could only watch as Alcindor scored 37 points and grabbed 20 rebounds in the title game. The year before, Alcindor scorched North Carolina for 34 points and 18 rebounds.

7. BOB KURLAND

Oklahoma State University won consecutive NCAA championships in 1945 and 1946 due to their towering 6′ 10″ center, Bob "Foothills" Kurland. He was the MVP in both tournaments. In the final game of the 1945 title game, Kurland scored 22 of his team's 49 points. The next year, Kurland scored 23 of his team's 43 points to lead them to a 43–40 win over North Carolina.

8. ALEX GROZA

In 1949 Alex Groza, Kentucky's All-American, led the Wildcats to a 46–36 win over Oklahoma State. Other players have scored more total points in a title game, but no player ever scored a higher percentage of his team's total points. Groza, a 6′ 7″ center, scored 25 points in the championship game, more than half his team's total points. Groza's dominance can be seen in that Kentucky's next highest scorers during the game scored only 5 points each.

9. CLYDE LOVELLETTE

In 1952 the University of Kansas defeated St. John's University 80–63 to capture the NCAA title. The Jayhawks rode the back of their 6′ 9″ center Clyde Lovellette. Lovellette, the nation's leading scorer during the regular season, did not disappoint in the final game. He scored 33 points and grabbed 17 rebounds. Lovellette went on to play in three National Basketball Association (NBA) All-Star games during an eleven-year professional career.

10. ARNIE FERRIN

In 1944 the University of Utah's so-called "Blitz Kids" defeated Dartmouth 42–40 in the first overtime title game in the tournament's history. Utah was led by their star freshman forward, Arnie Ferrin. He scored 22 of this team's 42 points to capture the tournament's top player award. Ironically, Utah was entered into the NCAA tournament only after the University of Arkansas had to pull out when several of its starters were injured in an automobile accident. Utah, which had lost in the National Invitation Tournament (NIT), accepted the substitute bid and made the most out of their second chance. Ferrin did not fare as well in the professional ranks, playing only three years for the Minneapolis Lakers.

Great Game 7s in NBA Finals

In the NBA Finals, a team has to win the best of seven games, or four games. Many times in NBA history a series final has been tied 3–3, with a deciding Game 7 in the balance. These players delivered in the clutch to enshrine themselves in NBA lore.

1. JAMES WORTHY 1988

The Los Angeles Lakers of the 1980s featured the "Showtime" attack of point guard Magic Johnson, center Kareem Abdul-Jabbar, and small forward James Worthy. In 1987 the Lakers captured the title by defeating the Celtics in six games. Coach Pat Riley guaranteed that his team would repeat. In the 1988 NBA Finals the Lakers proved Riley prescient, but not after a fierce fight from the Detroit Pistons. In Game 7, James Worthy lived up to his nickname of "Big Game James" by delivering one of the biggest games in NBA history. Worthy scored 36 points, grabbed 16 rebounds, and handed out 10 assists for a magnificent triple double. His final game heroics garnered him Finals MVP honors.

2. **WALT FRAZIER 1970**

In the 1970 NBA Finals, the New York Knicks squared off against the mighty Los Angeles Lakers, who were led by Wilt Chamberlain, Jerry West, and Elgin Baylor. The situation looked bleak for the Knicks after their star center Willis Reed injured his knee in Game 5. The mighty Chamberlain seized on Reed's absence from the action to dominate Game 6 and even the series. Most people remember Game 7 for Reed's historic entrance onto the court for the start of the game. Hobbling up and down the court, Reed nailed the first two shots of the game, which energized the Knicks. From there, Reed did not score again, but he didn't have to. The game belonged to the Knicks' fabulous point guard, Walt "Clyde" Frazier. Frazier scored 36 points, handed out an unbelievable 19 assists, and made 5 steals.

3. **BILL RUSSELL 1960**

In the 1960 NBA Finals, the Boston Celtics faced off against the St. Louis Hawks for the third time in four years. The rivalry featured some of the game's greatest players, such as the Celtics' point guard Bob Cousy and the Hawks' great power forward Bob Pettit. The Hawks won Game 6 in St. Louis to force a deciding Game 7 in Boston. In Game 7, the Celtics had many stars. None shone brighter than their center Bill Russell, who scored 22 points, grabbed an astonishing 35 rebounds, and dished out 4 assists.

4. **BILL RUSSELL 1962**

In the NBA Finals of the 1961–62 season, the mighty Boston Celtics faced off against their newest rivals, the Los Angeles Lakers. The growing Celtic dynasty met a stiff challenge from a talented Laker team that featured "Mr. Inside" Elgin Baylor and "Mr. Outside" Jerry West. In Game 5 in the finals Baylor scorched the Celtics for an NBA Finals–record of 61 points. In Game 7, the Celtics prevailed in a 110–107 overtime thriller. The dominant force was none other than the ultimate winner Bill Russell, who scored 30 points and grabbed an amazing 40 rebounds.

5.   BILL RUSSELL 1966

In 1966 the Boston Celtics were seeking their eighth straight NBA title. Standing in their way once again were the Los Angeles Lakers led by Elgin Baylor and Jerry West. In Game 7, the Celtics edged the Lakers 95–93. The dominant force yet again was Bill Russell, who scored 25 points and grabbed 32 rebounds.

6.   DAVE COWENS 1974

In the 1974 NBA Finals, Kareem Abdul-Jabbar led the Milwaukee Bucks against Dave Cowens's Boston Celtics. Milwaukee won Game 6 on a last-second skyhook shot by Abdul-Jabbar in double overtime. The series returned to Milwaukee for the final game. Cowens and the Celtics would not be denied, and they defeated the Bucks 102–87 behind Cowens's 28 points. It was perhaps the finest moment of Cowens's outstanding career.

7.   HAKEEM OLAJUWON 1994

In the 1994 NBA Finals, the Houston Rockets and New York Knicks engaged in a defensive lockdown. No team scored more than 100 points in any game. The Knicks, led by their great center Patrick Ewing, looked on the verge of a title after taking a 3–2 series lead.

However, the Rockets captured Game 6 to force the deciding game. In the final game, Rockets center Hakeem "The Dream" Olajuwon proved dominant once again. He tallied 25 points, 10 rebounds, 7 assists, and 3 blocks. Olajuwon captured his first NBA title and earned a measure of redemption against Ewing, who had defeated him for an NCAA title nearly ten years before in 1984.

8. CEDRIC MAXWELL 1984

The Boston Celtics and Los Angeles Lakers waged a pitched battle for NBA supremacy for much of the 1980s. The 1984 NBA Finals featured the premier rivalry in the sport between the Celtics' Larry Bird and the Lakers' Earvin "Magic" Johnson. Larry Bird outplayed Magic for much of the series, averaging 27 points and 14 rebounds per game. However, Game 7 featured the emergence of the Celtics' other starting forward, Cedric "Cornbread" Maxwell, the MVP of the Celtics' triumph over the Houston Rockets in the 1981 finals. In 1984 Maxwell, who had been quiet the entire series, erupted for a solid all-around game of 24 points, 8 rebounds, and 8 assists to lead his team to victory.

9. CONNIE HAWKINS 1968

Connie Hawkins entered the American Basketball Association (ABA) in its inaugural season at the age of 27. He had been banned by the NBA for his alleged association with gamblers. The ABA allowed Hawkins to play, and he dominated the league. He led the Pittsburgh Pipers to the championship against the New Orleans Buccaneers. In Game 7, Hawkins scored 20 points, grabbed 16 rebounds, and dished out 9 assists. It was a fitting end to an MVP season. Hawkins played one more year in the ABA before moving to the Phoenix Suns of the NBA, effectively lifting its ban on Hawkins.

10. ZELMO BEATY 1971

Zelmo Beaty was a star center in the NBA for several years before moving to the Utah Stars. His first year in the ABA, Beaty led the Stars to the championship round against the powerful Kentucky Colonels. In Game 7, Beaty scored 36 points and grabbed 16 rebounds to lead the Stars to a 131–121 triumph.

nCAA Upsets

The NCAA tournament may well be the crown jewel of basketball, generating so much excitement that it has been dubbed "March Madness." Since 1985, 64 teams are invited to participate in the tournament each year. The tournament is divided into four regions with 16 seeds in each region. Normally, higher seeded teams prevail—but not always. Every year there are teams that pull at least one upset, and the following are ten memorable upsets.

1. MTSU OVER KENTUCKY 1982

It was supposed to be the ultimate matchup of basketball powerhouses in the second round of the 1982 NCAA tournament in Nashville, Tennessee. Shirts were even printed featuring the pending showdown between Kentucky and Louisville. The problem was that someone forgot to tell the Middle Tennessee State University Blue Raiders and their fiery coach, Stan "Ramrod" Simpson. The Blue Raiders, a #11 seed, shocked a powerful Kentucky team led by future NBA players Dirk Minniefield and Melvin Turpin. Jerry Beck, the Ohio

Valley Conference (OVC) Player of the Year, led the Blue Raiders to an unbelievable 50–44 upset. Beck and freshman guard Edward "Pancakes" Perry played all forty minutes of the game. The Raiders hung with Louisville in the second-round game for a half before falling 81–56.

2. VILLANOVA OVER GEORGETOWN 1985

In 1985 the mighty Georgetown Hoyas, led by Player of the Year Patrick Ewing, were the odds-on choice to win the title. In fact they had won the championship the year before and were even better in 1985. In fact they were the best team in the country for most of the year. A #1 seed, the Hoyas manhandled a talented St. John's team in the semifinals to reach the championship game against another team from the Big East Conference (BEC)—the upstart Villanova Wildcats. Georgetown had defeated Villanova twice during the season, but Villanova appeared to be something of a team of destiny. It defeated Dayton by 2 points, Michigan by 4 points, and Maryland by 3 points in its first three tournament games. Most believed that Villanova's only chance of winning the title was to play a perfect game. The #8–seed Wildcats played a near-perfect game, missing only six field goal attempts the entire game. Villanova won 66–64.

3. NORTH CAROLINA STATE OVER HOUSTON 1983

The Houston Cougars were the most talented team in the country in 1983. The team—nicknamed Phi Slamma Jamma—featured future NBA Hall of Famers Hakeem "The Dream" Olajuwon and Clyde "The Glide" Drexler. It also featured Michael Young, Larry "Mr. Mean" Micheaux, Alvin Franklin, and the explosive Benny Anders. However, the Cougars faced a team of destiny led by Wolfpack coach Jimmy Valvano and his pair of experienced guards, Derrick Whittenburg and Sidney Lowe. North Carolina State squeaked out a first-round, double overtime win over Pepperdine and gradually improved with each game. It led Houston 33–25 at half-time and then withstood a Cougar second-half rally. With seconds remaining and the score tied 52–52, Whittenburg launched a 30-footer. The shot was an air ball but, with one second remaining, forward Lorenzo Charles slammed the ball home for an improbable 54–52 victory.

4. CANISIUS OVER NORTH CAROLINA STATE 1956

Heading into the 1956 NCAA tournament, North Carolina State looked primed to make a serious run at the national championship. The Wolfpack had compiled a formidable 24–3 season record and was ranked #2 in the country by the Associated Press. All that stood in its way in the first round on March 12, 1956, in Madison Square Garden, was tiny Canisius College from Buffalo, N.Y. However, Canisius outlasted North Carolina State 79–78 in four overtimes. The underdogs prevailed on a last-second shot by reserve Frank Corcoran.

5. PRINCETON OVER UCLA 1996

The UCLA Bruins won the 1995 NCAA championship, and they aimed to repeat their magic in 1996, as they faced the #13 seed Princeton Tigers of the Ivy League in the first round. Princeton coach Pete Carril was known as a basketball genius, but hardly anyone thought that the talented Bruins would lose the game. The #4 seeded Bruins led 41–34 with just more than five minutes to play; however, the Bruins would not score again. With seconds remaining, Princeton sophomore center Steve Goodrich fed freshman forward

Gabe Lewullis on a backdoor layup to win the game 43–41.

6. COPPIN STATE OVER SOUTH CAROLINA 1997

Only four times in NCAA history has a #15 seed defeated a #2 seed. In three of those games the final score was close. In the 1997 NCAA tournament, #15 seeded Coppin State dominated the #2 seed South Carolina 78–65. The Gamecocks were rated #6 in the country with the talented trio of B. J. McKie, Melvin Watson, and Larry Davis. Still, Antoine Brockingham and Terquinn Mott led the Pirates to a stunning upset.

7. UAB OVER KENTUCKY 1981

In 2004 the University of Alabama-Birmingham (UAB) surprised Kentucky in a second-round upset. But 23 years earlier, UAB pulled an even more shocking surprise. In 1981 it was the Ides of March for the mighty Kentucky "Big Blue" basketball team. In the second round of the NCAA tournament, UAB defeated the Wildcats 69–62 on March 15. The victory was especially remarkable given that UAB was in only its third year of basketball competition. Led by star guard Oliver Robinson, the team's first full basketball scholarship athlete, and coach Gene Bartow, UAB pulled the upset led by Robinson's game-high 18 points.

8. MTSU OVER FLORIDA STATE 1989

In the 1989 NCAA tournament, the powerful Florida State Seminoles featured a lethal offensive scoring punch led by star guard and future NBA three-point specialist George McCloud. The heavily-favored Seminoles were a huge favorite over the #13-seeded Middle Tennessee State Blue Raiders, and the Seminoles dominated the action for much of the game. In fact, at one point they led by 17 points in the second half. Then a strange thing happened. MTSU freshman Mike Buck caught fire from long range, connecting on four straight three-pointers in one stretch. Buck scored 23 of his game-high 26 points in the second half to lead the Blue Raiders to a shocking upset, with a final score of 97–83. Buck never matched his one-game magic in an otherwise mediocre four-year career.

9. CLEVELAND STATE OVER INDIANA 1986

In the 1986 NCAA tournament, Cleveland State, the #14 seed in the East region, shocked national power Indiana, the number #3 seed, by a score of 83–79. The upstart Vikings posted a record of 27–3 coming into the tournament, but most experts thought that Indiana, with star guard Steve Alford and fiery head coach Bob Knight, would prevail. Instead, the Vikings used their superior speed to press the entire game and force the action. Led by freshman guard Ken "Mouse" McFadden, Cleveland State did not stop after defeating Indiana. They beat St. Joseph's in the second round to advance to the Sweet Sixteen, where they narrowly lost to a David Robinson–led Navy team by 1 point.

10. SANTA CLARA OVER ARIZONA 1993

In the 1993 NCAA tournament, Arizona looked to redeem itself after losing to #14 East Tennessee State in the 1992 tournament. This time Arizona was a 20-point favorite over the Santa Clara Broncos, a team that had limped to a 15–11 regular season record. However, the #15-seed Broncos paid no attention to the oddsmakers and shocked the #2 seed 64–61 behind star point guard Steve Nash.

Freshman Phenoms

For many years, freshman were not allowed to compete on college varsity squads. The freshman eligibility rule was designed to give youngsters a chance to adapt to the rigors of the college academic environment. In 1973, the NCAA changed course and allowed freshman to compete in athletics. These players took advantage of the rule change and made huge impacts on their schools' basketball programs. As such, they deserve the billing of freshman phenoms.

1. JAMES "FLY" WILLIAMS

The first year that freshman were allowed to play in years was 1973, and what a year it was for former New York City playground legend James "Fly" Williams and the tiny OVC team called Austin Peay University. Assistant coach Leonard Hamilton convinced Williams to come to the school in Clarksville, Tennessee. Williams had an immediate and indelible impact on the Austin Peay program and the Lake Kelly–coached team. He set a freshman scoring record, averaging a league-best

29.4 points per game. For his remarkable scoring efforts, Williams earned OVC Player of the Year honors. He led Austin Peay to their first-ever NCAA tournament, including a 77–75 win over Jacksonville. Williams then led his team to a near-upset of the powerful Kentucky Wildcats, who prevailed 106–100 in overtime.

2. CHRIS JACKSON

Louisiana State University has had its share of basketball greats, including such luminaries as Bob Pettit, "Pistol" Pete Maravich, and Shaquille O'Neal. Also worthy of mention on this exclusive list is none other than Chris Jackson. The mercurial point guard from Gulfport, Mississippi, took the Southeastern Conference (SEC) by storm by averaging a league-best 30.2 points per game. In December, Jackson amazed college basketball experts with a 53-point outburst against Florida. His efforts earned him Southeastern Conference (SEC) MVP honors. Jackson still holds the NCAA career scoring record by a freshman. He later changed his name to Mahmoud Abdul-Rauf and played in the NBA.

3. CARMELO ANTHONY

In 2003, Carmelo Anthony took the Big East and college basketball by storm. He led the Syracuse Orangeman to an improbable NCAA championship, and in the Final Four, Anthony took it to an even higher level. He scored a career-high 33 points against Texas in the semifinals. He added 20 points, 10 rebounds, and 7 assists in the title game against Kansas, and was only the third freshman ever named the MOP of an NCAA Final Four.

4. JASON KIDD

In 1993, point guard prodigy Jason Kidd led the University of California Bearcats to the NCAA tournament. Kidd earned Pacific-10 (PAC-10) Freshman of the Year honors with 13 points and nearly 8 assists per game. He also set an NCAA record for a freshman by averaging 3.79 steals per contest. In the Big Dance, Kidd led his team to a stunning 82–77 win over two-time NCAA defending champions, the Duke Blue Devils.

5. PERVIS ELLISON

Pervis Ellison entered the national spotlight in 1986 as a freshman center for the Louisville Cardinals. Nicknamed "Never Nervous," Ellison lived up to his nickname in the NCAA tournament as he handled the pressure of the moment better than any other player on the court. He led the Cardinals to the national championship with a 72–69 win over the Duke Blue Devils. Ellison scored 25 points and grabbed 11 rebounds on his way to earning Final Four MOP honors.

6. JAY EDWARDS

Jay Edwards earned Big 10 Freshman of the Year honors in 1988 for his sterling play at Indiana University. He led the Hoosiers to the Big 10 title with last-second shots over Purdue and Michigan. Among his many accomplishments that year, Edwards set an NCAA record that still stands by averaging 53.6% from three-point territory.

7. SIDNEY MONCRIEF

Sidney Moncrief was a 6′ 4″ junior guard/forward who led the University of Arkansas Razorbacks to the 1978

Final Four. Moncrief was spectacular as a freshman in 1976 when he averaged 66.5% from the field, an unbeaten NCAA record.

8. KENNY ANDERSON

New York high school basketball legend Kenny Anderson lived up to his billing when he earned national Freshman of the Year honors for Georgia Tech in 1990. He also received all-conference honors in the Atlantic Coast Conference (ACC). Anderson triggered the Yellow Jackets' potent offensive attack—known as Lethal Weapon III for its three main stars Anderson, Brian Oliver, and Dennis Scott. Anderson guided his team to the Final Four, where they lost to the eventual champion UNLV.

9. BERNARD KING

Bernard King dominated college basketball the day he stepped on the court for the University of Tennessee Volunteers. In his first college game in November 1974, King scored 42 points against Wisconsin-Milwaukee. King averaged better than 26 points per game on his way to earning SEC Player of the Year honors in 1975 as a freshman.

10. FAB FIVE

The 1991 recruiting class of the University of Michigan Wolverines' basketball squad was one of the most heralded of all time. The so-called Fab Five included Chris Webber, Juwan Howard, Jalen Rose, Jimmy King, and Ray Jackson. The Fab Five earned their place in college basketball history by becoming the first team in NCAA history to make it to the championship game with five freshman starters. They led the defending champion Duke Blue Devils 31–30 at halftime but faltered in the second half, losing 71–51.

They Played Great in College But Not in the Pros

Oftentimes great college basketball players turn into outstanding professionals. Pete Maravich led college basketball in scoring for three straight years at LSU, and then also had success in the NBA (though not as much as he had in college).

However, other players often reach the pinnacle of success at the college level but cannot reach the same level of greatness in the pros. These ten players dominated college basketball but had less than awe-inspiring professional careers.

1. **BUTCH LEE**

Butch Lee had a great college career at Marquette, including a major role in leading the team to the 1977 national championship with a 67–59 win over North Carolina. Lee garnered MOP of the Final Four for his efforts, and the next year he won the Naismith Award as college basketball's finest player. However, Lee could not match such accomplishments in the NBA.

Lee played only 96 games over two seasons with three different teams. He averaged only 8 points per game.

2. **KEITH LEE**

Keith Lee had one of the greatest college basketball careers in his four years at Memphis State. Lee scored more than 2,400 points and grabbed 1,330 rebounds, and he was a three-time All-American. The Chicago Bulls selected Lee at number eleven in the first round of the 1985 draft. Unfortunately, Lee's sore knees made him a bust in the NBA. He played only three seasons, garnering anemic averages of 6.1 points and 4.7 rebounds per game.

3. **JOHNNY NEUMANN**

Johnny Neumann—or Carl John Neumann—was a tremendous scorer for the University of Mississippi in his sophomore season of 1971. Neumann led the nation in scoring at a remarkable clip of 40.1 points per game. His season included a 48-point outburst against the Kentucky Wildcats and their legendary coach Adolph Rupp. Neumann left after his sophomore year, signing with the Memphis Pros of the ABA. He had a few good years of scoring, as in his second season when he averaged 19.2 points per game. But Neumann is remembered more for what he did not do on the court than for his contribution. Many consider him a wasted talent because he failed to stay in proper shape and played poor defense. Fellow ABA player Dave Twardzik said in Terry Pluto's *Loose Balls* that "it always bothered me that Johnny Neumann never was the player he should have been." Neumann has had a successful career as a coach of minor professional league and foreign teams. He twice led teams to the Continental Basketball

Marquette University Archives

Butch Lee.

Association (CBA) championship game, and has also coached in Germany, Greece, Belgium, and Lebanon.

4. RICK MOUNT

Rick Mount was an Indiana high school basketball legend who, in 1966, became the first high schooler to ever grace the cover of *Sports Illustrated*. He graduated from Lebanon High School in Lebanon, Indiana, with nearly 2,600 career points. He continued his scoring assault at Purdue University, where he scored more than 2,300 points in three years for a career scoring average of 32.3 points per game. However, Mount's pro career never amounted to the hype he generated in high school and college. He signed with the Indiana Pacers out of the ABA, but lasted only two years there. His career scoring average in his five-year professional career was only 11.2 points per game. His final scoring total was 3,330 points, and he retired at the age of 28.

5. JEFF LAMP

Jeff Lamp had a great college basketball career scoring more than 2,300 points from 1977–1981 for the University of Virginia Cavaliers. The school retired Lamp's number because of his great career, but Lamp flopped in the NBA. Drafted in the first round at number fifteen by the Portland Trailblazers, Lamp never made an impact. He posted a pathetic career scoring average of 1.5 points per game.

6. KENT BENSON

Kent Benson had a great career with Indiana University from 1973–1977, scoring more than 1,700 points and grabbing more than 1,000 rebounds. Part of Indiana's undefeated championship team in 1976, Benson won the Final Four MOP award for his stellar play. The Milwaukee Bucks selected Benson with the overall number one pick in the 1977 NBA draft. Benson had a journeyman's career in the NBA, posting career averages of 9.1 points and 5.7 rebounds per game.

7. SCOTT MAY

Scott May scored nearly 1,600 points for the Indiana Hoosiers from 1973–76. He won the Naismith Award in 1976 as college basketball's finest player, and his efforts led the Chicago Bulls to select him as the number two pick in the 1976 NBA draft. May's NBA career began with promise when he averaged 14.6 points per game in his rookie season. However, that was as good as it got for May in the NBA. In four of his seven NBA seasons he did not even average double figures. Perhaps his son Sean, who led North Carolina to the 2005 NCCA title, will have a better NBA career.

8. WALTER BERRY

Walter Berry was considered by most experts to be the best college basketball player during the 1986 season. In his sophomore season in 1985, he helped Chris Mullin lead St. John's to the Final Four. The following year, Berry averaged 23 points per game and dominated the interior with his amazing assortment of inside spin moves. As a collegian, Berry lived up to his nickname of "The Truth." He won the prestigious Wooden Award as a junior, left school after his junior year, and was selected in the first round at number fourteen by the Portland Trailblazers. He played three NBA seasons with four teams. He averaged as much as 17 points per game and shot 56.3% from the field in 1986–87, but his defense was lacking. Berry left to play professional basketball in Europe where he had some great years in Italy and Spain, but he never reached his potential in the NBA.

9. ALFREDRICK HUGHES

Alfredrick Hughes was one of college basketball's all-time great scorers. Playing for Loyola-Chicago from 1981–85, Hughes tallied more than 2,900 career points. He led Loyola to the Sweet Sixteen and was named the Midwestern Collegiate Conference (MCC) Player of the Year three times. The San Antonio Spurs selected Hughes in the first round at number fifteen, but he never made an NBA roster and never played in an NBA game.

10. LARUE MARTIN

Another product of Loyola-Chicago proved to have a great college basketball career but little success in the professional ranks. Larue Martin played at Loyola from 1969–72, scoring more than 1,200 points and grabbing 1,072 rebounds in three seasons. One year, he scored 18.7 points and grabbed more than 17 rebounds a game. In 1972, the Portland Trailblazers made one of the NBA draft's biggest blunders (as mentioned in the original *Basketball's Most Wanted*™) by selecting Martin as the number one pick. Martin played only four seasons and posted anemic averages of 5.3 points and 4.6 rebounds.

Transfer Talents

Sometimes college players just want a change of scenery. Whether it's a personality difference with a coach or a desire for greater playing time, many players leave for what they feel will be greener pastures. For example, Kentucky great Kyle Macy actually played his freshman year at Purdue University before transferring and finding success in the Bluegrass State. These players all made great impacts on their new teams.

1. ELGIN BAYLOR

Elgin Baylor, dubbed "the man of a thousand moves," dazzled fans in the NBA for many years, earning acclaim as one of the greatest players ever. But Baylor was not a known commodity coming out of Washington, D.C., as a high school player. In fact, he went to the College of Idaho to play football. Baylor played basketball for one year at the College of Idaho, and averaged more than 30 points per game. Baylor then transferred to Seattle University. In the 1957–58 season, Baylor took Seattle all the way to the NCAA championship game against the University of Kentucky.

Although Kentucky defeated Seattle 84–72, Baylor was named the tournament's MOP. In his last season at Seattle, Baylor averaged 32.5 points per game and 19.3 rebounds per game.

2. LAWRENCE ROBERTS

Power forward Lawrence Roberts starred at Baylor University his first two years of college where he led the team in scoring and rebounding. He was an all-conference selection both years. However, in 2003, the Baylor program was rocked by tragedy and scandal. Baylor player Brian Dennehy was found murdered, and another Baylor player was charged with the crime. Furthermore, Baylor's coach at the time, Dave Bliss, resigned after facing intense scrutiny related to the running of the program. Normally transfers have to sit out a year before playing for a new school, but in light of the highly unusual circumstances, the NCAA made a special exemption for players who transferred from Baylor. Roberts transferred to the Mississippi State Bulldogs in Starkville, Mississippi. He made an immediate impact, leading the team in scoring and rebounding. His on-court accomplishments earned him SEC Player of the Year honors for 2003–04. He led the Bulldogs back to NCAA tournament in his senior year in 2004–05.

3. BILLY McCAFFREY

Billy McCaffrey surprised many college basketball experts when he transferred from the defending champion Duke Blue Devils to the Vanderbilt Commodores. McCaffrey played a key role in Duke's championship squad in 1990–91. He averaged 11.6 points per game and earned NCAA All-Tournament honors. Still,

McCaffrey transferred to Vanderbilt, ostensibly to receive more playing time and the chance to play point guard. The transfer turned out well for McCaffrey and Vanderbilt. In his first year there, McCaffrey averaged 20.6 points per game, earned co-MVP of the SEC, and led the Commodores to a national ranking and the Sweet Sixteen. His senior year, he also averaged more than 20 points per game and led the Commodores to the NIT championship game.

4. TRAVIS FORD

Travis Ford played high school basketball in Madisonville, Kentucky, earning Parade All-American honors for his play. However, he signed to play for the University of Missouri because the University of Kentucky did not recruit him. He stayed at Missouri for only year before he transferred to Kentucky. In his junior and senior seasons of 1992–93 and 1993–94, Ford earned First-Team All SEC honors and MVP of the SEC tournament twice. Ford, though standing only 5′ 9″, had a large impact on the game with his deadly three-point shooting. Coach Rick Pitino called him one of the best shooters he had ever seen. Ford served as the head coach at Eastern Kentucky University until the end of the 2004–05 season. He now coaches at the University of Massachusetts.

5. JOHN LUCAS III

John Lucas III, the son of University of Maryland and NBA great John Lucas, scored more than 3,000 points in a great high school career in Houston, Texas. He signed up to play for Baylor University. He played there for two years, averaging 12 and 13 points per game each season as the team's point guard. However,

Lucas transferred in 2003 after the murder of Brian Dennehy and the resulting scandal with the school's basketball program. Lucas transferred to Oklahoma State, where he earned Big 12 First Team All-Conference honors. Lucas's heady play and last-second heroics guided the Cowboys all the way to the Final Four.

6. JAMES "SCOONIE" PENN

Point guard Scoonie Penn signed with Boston College after a great high school career in Salem, Massachusetts. Penn made an immediate impact with the Eagles in 1995–96, earning Big East Rookie of the Year honors. The next year he led the Eagles to the Big East tournament title. However, Boston College's coach Jim O'Brien left the school to take over the head job at Ohio State University. Penn transferred to OSU in large part to play for his coach. After sitting out a year, Penn performed even better than before. In the 1998–99 season, Penn earned Big 10 Player of the Year, became an All-American and led the Buckeyes to the Final Four. Penn's transfer helped the Buckeyes make one of the most dramatic one-year turnarounds in NCAA history. The year Penn sat out the Buckeyes endured a miserable 8–22 record. In Penn's first year of play the team made the Final Four.

7. DAN DICKAU

Dan Dickau's two seasons with the University of Washington left him unsatisfied. In his freshman year he didn't see much playing time, while an injury cut short a promising sophomore campaign. Dickau transferred after the 1998–99 season to Gonzaga, which ran a more up-tempo offense and had achieved recent success in the NCAA tournament. Dickau prospered under

Gonzaga's fast-paced offensive system. He averaged more than 20 points per game in his two seasons with Gonzaga, and he became a first-round pick in the 2002 NBA draft.

8. DARRYL BEDFORD

Darryl Bedford, a 6′ 8″, 260-plus pound forward who shot three-pointers like a shotputter, began his college career at the University of Arkansas—on the bench. In two years at Arkansas he averaged less than 10 minutes per game and less than 3 points per game. Bedford transferred to Austin Peay University in Clarksville, Tennessee. After sitting out the 1984–85 season, he played his final two years for the Governors. Bedford saved his best for last, averaging more than 16 points per game in his senior year. He led Austin Peay to the OVC tournament title, earning MVP honors and his team an automatic NCAA bid.

In the Big Dance, Bedford and his teammates looked like they were headed for an early exit when they, as the #14 seed, were paired against the #3 seed Illinois. At halftime the game was tied 32–32, and announcer Dick Vitale declared that if the Governors won the game he would "stand on his head." The burly Bedford shocked Vitale, the Illini, and much of the college basketball world by nailing five three-pointers and racking up 24 points. True to his word, Vitale later stood on his head. The Governors lost in the next round to the Providence Friars in overtime, after Bedford fouled out of the game.

9. DEREK ANDERSON

Swingman Derek Anderson played his first two years of college ball at Ohio State University. After the program went through much adversity in coach Randy Ayers's final years, Anderson looked for greener pastures. He found them in the Bluegrass State, playing for Rick Pitino's Kentucky Wildcats. In his first year playing for the Wildcats, Kentucky captured the national championship with a victory over Syracuse. In his senior season Anderson averaged more than 17 points per game, until he suffered a season-ending knee injury. His injury likely cost the Wildcats a back-to-back national title, as they lost to Arizona in the final game in overtime. A healthy Kentucky squad with Anderson in the lineup likely would have won the game. Anderson now plays in the NBA with the Portland Trailblazers.

10. **LARRY FOGLE**

Larry Fogle began his college basketball career as a freshman at the University of Southwestern Louisiana. He transferred after one year to Canisius University. The transfer seemed to pay dividends for Fogle, and he led the nation in scoring in his sophomore season (1973–74) with an average of 33.4 points per game. In 1975–76 Fogle played only two games for the New York Knicks. He played minor league pro ball after that, but never played again in the NBA.

Played For One Team

Most NBA players ply their craft for multiple teams during their career. Every so often, a player—often the franchise's star player—will stay with the same team for an entire career. For instance, Patrick Ewing came to symbolize the New York Knicks for much of the 1980s and 1990s, amassing 16 seasons with the squad. However, as with many superstars, Ewing also played a season or two with another team when he was well past his prime. These ten players played their entire career for the same team.

1. JOHN STOCKTON

John Stockton played nineteen seasons for the same team—an NBA record. In 1984, the Utah Jazz drafted Stockton in the first round. Many experts laughed at the Jazz for taking Stockton, who was a relative unknown from a then-obscure school called Gonzaga. Stockton proved his critics wrong, retiring in 2003 as the NBA's all-time leader in assists and steals.

2. REGGIE MILLER

The 2004–05 season was Reggie Miller's eighteenth NBA season, and his eighteenth with the Indiana Pacers.

Drafted in 1987 out of UCLA, Miller has terrorized opposing defenses with his clutch three-point shooting and non-stop movement without the ball. He is the NBA's all-time leader in three-point shooting, and he has scored more than 25,000 career points.

3. JOHN HAVLICEK

John Havlicek played all sixteen of his NBA seasons with the Boston Celtics from 1962 to his retirement in 1978. During his tenure, the team won eight NBA titles, and he scored more than 26,000 points. He played in thirteen All-Star games and was named First Team All-Defense five times. He was elected to the Hall of Fame in 1983.

4. LARRY BIRD

Larry Legend donned the Celtic green and white for all thirteen of his NBA seasons. To many, Bird epitomized Celtic pride, leading the team to NBA titles in 1981, 1984, and 1986. Bird earned twelve trips to the NBA All-Star game in his career.

5. MICHAEL COOPER

Michael Cooper terrorized offensive players for twelve seasons in the NBA, all with the Los Angeles Lakers. He was selected to the NBA All-Defensive Team numerous times. His playing days over, Cooper now is an assistant coach with the Denver Nuggets.

6. FRED BROWN

"Downtown" Fred Brown played for the Seattle Supersonics all thirteen years of his NBA career, which spanned from 1971 until 1984. Brown was known for his nearly unlimited range. In the 1975–76 season he averaged more than 23 points per game. He played in one All-Star game and scored more than 14,000 points in his career.

7. EARVIN "MAGIC" JOHNSON

Earvin "Magic" Johnson played thirteen seasons for the Los Angeles Lakers, and led the team to five NBA championships. Johnson personified the Lakers' "Showtime" fast break with his pinpoint passing and clutch performances. Johnson played twelve straight seasons from 1979 to 1991, retiring after he discovered he was HIV-positive. Johnson later returned to the Lakers for part of the 1995–96 season.

8. DAVID ROBINSON

David Robinson anchored the San Antonio Spurs franchise for fourteen NBA seasons, from 1989 until his retirement in 2003. Robinson could have added two more seasons to his career, but he had to spend two years in the United States Navy after graduating from the Naval Academy. Known as "The Admiral," Robinson became the face of the Spurs franchise. His coach Gregg Popovich said it best: "I have never been around a more remarkable human being."

9. BYRON BECK

Byron Beck has a strong connection to the city of Denver; he played college basketball at Denver University. He didn't have to move very far when he graduated to the professional ranks because he stayed in Denver to play for the ABA's Nuggets. He played all nine years of the ABA's existence with the Nuggets and one year after the Nuggets moved to the NBA.

10. **TOM BOERWINKLE**

Tom Boerwinkle dominated the paint with his 7' frame at the University of Tennessee. He started with the Chicago Bulls in 1968 and did not retire until 1978. In his ten-year NBA career, Boerwinkle averaged double figures in two seasons.

They Coached One College Team

Normally, college coaches get their start at the high school level or as an assistant coach at a university. Coaches will often work at several universities before finding their dream jobs. However, a special few coaches have landed at one college and stayed there for their entire careers. Such was the case for the following ten coaches.

1. ADOLPH RUPP

"The Baron of the Bluegrass," Adolph Rupp coached for forty-one years at the University of Kentucky, from 1931–1972. Rupp coached at high schools in Kansas, Iowa, and Illinois before being hired as the coach of Kentucky in May 1930. He was only twenty-nine years old. He won 876 games and lost only 190, and his teams won four national championships.

2. RAY MEYER

Ray Meyer ran the squad at DePaul University as head coach for forty-two seasons from 1943–1984. He assumed the head-coaching position after serving as an assistant coach during the 1941–42 season. Meyer never won a national championship but took his teams to thirteen NCAA and eight NIT tournaments. Two of his teams, in 1943 and 1979, made the Final Four. Upon his retirement, his son Joey Meyer became the new head coach of DePaul.

3. **DON HASKINS**

Don Haskins coached at Texas-El Paso (formerly Texas Western) for thirty-eight seasons from 1962–1999. Previously, he coached high school basketball in Benjamin, Texas, and then at Hedley High School in Hedley, Texas. Haskins's greatest moment came in the 1966 NCAA championship game when his Texas Western squad, which started five African American players, defeated Adolph Rupp's all-white Kentucky squad 72–65 to win the title.

4. **ED DIDDLE**

Ed Diddle became the head basketball coach of Western Kentucky in 1923 after coaching two years of high school ball. Diddle never left the Hilltoppers, coaching there until 1964. He won 759 games and lost 302. His teams made three NCAA tournaments. Diddle was known for carrying a red towel that he would throw into the air when protesting an official's call.

5. **PAUL D. "TONY" HINKLE**

Tony Hinkle graduated from the University of Chicago and lettered in basketball, football, and baseball. After his graduation, he was hired to coach all three sports at Butler University in Indiana. Hinkle coached at Butler from 1927–1942 and again from 1946–1970. His coaching career was only interrupted by his service in the Navy during World War II. In 1965, Butler's gymnasium was renamed Hinkle Fieldhouse. He won 591 games in his coaching career.

6. DEAN SMITH

The legendary Dean Smith coached at the University of North Carolina for thirty-six seasons from 1962–1997. He led UNC to thirteen ACC championships, eleven Final Fours, and two national titles in 1982 and 1993. His teams made a record twenty-three consecutive trips to the NCAA tournament. Before assuming the mantle at North Carolina, he served as assistant coach there from 1958 through 1961.

7. GUY LEWIS

Guy Lewis played basketball at the University of Houston and graduated in 1947. He returned to the school as an assistant coach in 1953, and in 1957 he became head coach, where he remained for thirty seasons until 1986. He led his teams to five Final Fours, but he was never able to win an NCAA title. He was named the Associated Press's National Coach of the Year twice, in 1968 and 1983.

8. DENNY CRUM

Denny Crum coached for thirty years at the University of Louisville from 1972–2000. He won two national championships in 1980 and 1986, and he coached six teams that went to the Final Four. Before assuming the head job at Louisville, Crum was an assistant coach at his alma mater UCLA under the legendary John Wooden. He also coached junior college basketball in Los Angeles.

9. AMORY T. "SLATS" GILL

Amory T. "Slats" Gill was head coach at Oregon State University from 1929–1964, the only college head coaching position he held. He coached two years of high school basketball in Oakland, California, and then he was the coach for Oregon State's freshman team. As head coach, he compiled a record of 599 wins and 392 losses. His teams made two Final Fours, in 1949 and 1963. The coliseum on Oregon State's campus is named in Gill's honor.

10. WARD L. "PIGGY" LAMBERT

Ward L. "Piggy" Lambert coached high school basketball after doing graduate work at the University of Minnesota. In 1916, he became head coach at Purdue University. After serving in World War I, Lambert returned to Purdue in 1919 where he coached until 1942. He compiled a record of 351 wins and 172 losses. His 1931–32 squad went 17–1 and was named national champions by the Helms Athletic Foundation.

Three-Point Kings (NBA)

In 1979, the NBA adopted the three-point shot. The shot has become a staple in the league, as teams like the Sacramento Kings and Dallas Mavericks have used the three-point shot as a fearsome offensive weapon. These ten NBA players are perhaps best known for their ability to nail the three-pointer.

1. REGGIE MILLER

No one has hit more three-pointers in the history of the NBA than the Indiana Pacers' Reggie Miller, who has nailed more than 2,400 in his career. During the 1996–97 season Miller hit an amazing 229 three-pointers. He also is the NBA's all-time three-point king in playoff games, with more than 300 shots. Most impressive, though, is Miller's uncanny knack for nailing treys in the clutch.

2. LARRY BIRD

Larry Bird won the NBA's first Long Distance Shootout competition in 1986. Bird won the three-point competition all three years he entered, from 1986 until 1988.

Bird led the league in successful three-pointers during the 1985–86 season with 82. Many consider Bird one of the greatest, if not the greatest, shooter in NBA history.

3. CRAIG HODGES

Craig Hodges earned fame for his three-point shooting while he was a member of the Chicago Bulls. Hodges captured the NBA's Long Distance Shootout award in three consecutive years, from 1990 until 1992. He is the only man besides Larry Bird to win three such competitions in a row. At one point during the competition, he nailed an amazing 19 consecutive three-pointers. He has hit more than 500 three-pointers in NBA regular season games.

4. FRED BROWN

"Downtown" Freddie Brown achieved this nickname for his patented long range bombs as a guard for the Seattle Supersonics. Brown was a streak shooter with unlimited range. During the 1979–80, the first year the NBA adopted the three-point rule, Brown led the league in three-point field goal averages.

5. STEVE KERR

Steve Kerr parlayed his deft outside shooting touch into a seventeen-year NBA career that netted him five championship rings—three with the Chicago Bulls and two with the San Antonio Spurs. Kerr's role was to provide deadly outside shooting. In the 1994–95 season, Kerr hit an amazing 52.4% of his three-pointers. The next year he hit 51.5% of his treys. In his last year in the league, Kerr became a surprise hero for the San Antonio Spurs during the Western Conference Championships against the Dallas Mavericks, when he came off the bench to hit four three-pointers. Kerr's unlikely emergence enabled the Spurs to advance to the NBA Finals.

6. DALE ELLIS

Dale Ellis played seventeen years in the NBA for six different teams. His trademark was consistent, long-range bombing. Ellis won the NBA's Long Distance Shootout competition in 1989. Ironically, the 6′ 7″ Ellis scored the majority of his points in the paint while starring for the University of Tennessee Volunteers. In the professional ranks, Ellis changed his game. He hit a total of 1,703 three pointers for an amazing career average of 40.3%.

7. TIM LEGLER

Tim Legler earned his spot on an NBA roster for several years because of his accurate jump shot. His best year came during the 1995–96 season when he hit 52.2% of his three-pointers. That year he captured the NBA's Long Distance Shootout competition during All-Star Weekend. Legler defeated Orlando's Dennis Scott 20–14 in the final round.

8. GLEN RICE

Glen Rice was one of the best pure shooters in NBA history, tallying more than 1,500 three-pointers from 1989 until his retirement during the 2003–04 season. During the 1996–97 season for the Charlotte Hornets, Rice hit 207 three-pointers and shot 47% from behind the arc. Rice captured the NBA's Long Distance Shootout competition during All-Star Weekend in 1995.

9. **CHRIS FORD**

On October 12, 1979, Chris Ford of the Boston Celtics hit the NBA's first three-pointer in league history. That year, Ford hit 70 of 164 trey attempts for 42.7%. Ford's career three-point totals do not reflect his ability as a shooter because he played seven full NBA seasons before the league adopted the three-point rule.

10. **PEJA STOJAKOVIC**

Peja Stojakovic of the Sacramento Kings is considered by many experts to be the best shooter in the NBA today. Twice at All-Star Weekend, in 2002 and 2003, Peja won the Long Distance Shootout competition. In 2004, he finished second. For his career, Stojakovic has averaged nearly 40% from the three-point line.

Three-Point Kings
(NCAA)

C ollege basketball instituted the three-point shot on a wide-scale basis in 1986, but it was used experimentally before that. On February 7, 1945, Columbia and Fordham played a game with a twenty-one-foot three-point line. The teams combined for 20 "long goals," as they were then called. Columbia won the game 73–58. Then in 1980, the Southern Conference instituted the three-point line for a season. On November 29, 1980, Western Carolina's Ronnie Carr nailed a three-pointer against Middle Tennessee State University. Now, the three-point line is a regular staple of the game. The following ten individuals were noteworthy for their three-point marksmanship in college.

1. **CURTIS STAPLES**

Curtis Staples scored 1,757 points for the University of Virginia from 1994–98. More than 1,200 of those points came from behind the long-distance arc, as Staples nailed 413 three-pointers in his 122-game career. He is college basketball's all-time leader in successful three-pointers.

2. DARRIN FITZGERALD

Darrin Fitzgerald was a senior guard for Butler University when college basketball introduced the three-point rule change. Though he only had one year to play under the rule, Fitzgerald made the most of it. He nailed 158 three-pointers in the 1986–87 season for an unbeaten NCAA record, averaging an amazing 5.64 three-pointers per game.

3. TERRENCE WOODS

Terrence Woods of Florida A&M nailed 139 three-pointers during his junior season (2002–03), and 140 three-pointers during his senior season (2003–04). In March 2004, Woods won college basketball's Three-Point Challenge, defeating Oregon's Luke Jackson 23–20 in the final round.

4. GLENN TROPF

In the 1987–88 season, Holy Cross's junior guard Glenn Tropf nailed 52 of 82 three-point shots for an amazing 63.4%. The record still stands as the best success rate in the history of NCAA Division I basketball.

5. JEFF FRYER

On March 18, 1990, Loyola Marymount's Jeff Fryer connected on 11 three-pointers in his team's upset of defending national champion Michigan in the second round of the NCAA tournament. In the tournament the year before, Fryer set another NCAA record when he attempted 23 three-point field goals in a single game against Arkansas. He finished his college career with 363 three-pointers.

6. KEITH VENEY

On December 14, 1996, Marshall University's Keith Veney nailed 15 three-pointers in a game versus Morehead State. With that rash of long bombs, Veney set an NCAA record for the most three-pointers in a single game.

7. FREDDIE BANKS

During the 1986–87 season, UNLV's Freddie Banks nailed 152 three-pointers in 39 games. In a Final Four game against Indiana University, Banks hit 11 of 19 three-pointers to keep the game close against the Hoosiers, who went on to win the NCAA title that year.

8. DENNIS SCOTT

Dennis Scott was one of the NBA's best three-pointer shooters, hitting ten in a single game. However, Scott was also deadly behind the arc in college for the Georgia Tech Yellow Jackets. In 1990, Scott led the nation with 137 three-pointers.

9. TONY BENNETT

For his college career, Tony Bennett of Wisconsin–Green Bay connected on 290 out of 584 three-pointers for a career 49.8%. No player who has made at least 200 treys has ever shot a better percentage.

10. BRUCE SEALS

Manhattan's Bruce Seals could be dubbed the Mad Bomber, at least for one game against Canisius on Jan. 31, 2000. He nailed 9 out of 27 three-pointers in the game on his way to 41 points. However, Canisius won the game 105–98 in the fourth overtime.

Court Thieves

An old saying claims that defense wins champion-ships. A key part of an effective defense is forcing the other team to turn the ball over, and one way to force turnovers is to steal the ball from the opponent. These players made a habit of thievery on the court.

1. DESMOND CAMBRIDGE

Desmond Cambridge set an NCAA record in 2002 for most steals in a season when he made an incredible 160 steals in 29 games as a senior guard for Alabama A&M. Cambridge's phenomenal season amounted to 5.52 steals per game—more than many teams average. Cambridge also owns the all-time career record for average steals per game at 3.93. In 2005, Cambridge played for the Nashville Rhythm of the ABA.

2. MOOKIE BLAYLOCK

Mookie Blaylock was consistently among the leaders in steals at both the college and pro levels. In his two years at the University of Oklahoma, Blaylock nabbed 281 steals for an average of 3.8 per game—second

A. Carlton Rice, Huntsville, AL

Desmond Cambridge.

only to Desmond Cambridge. He set the NCAA record for the most steals in a single game at 13, in games against Centenary and Loyola Marymount. As a professional ballplayer, Blaylock snagged 2,075 steals with a career average of 2.33 per game.

3. JOHN LINEHAM

John Lineham stood only 5′ 9″, but he stood tall at Providence with his knack for taking the ball away from his opponents. Lineham is the NCAA's career leader in total steals with 385.

4. EDWIN "GREEDY" DANIELS

Edwin "Greedy" Daniels had to be included in this list, if for no other reason than his nickname. On December 30, 2000, Daniels—a guard for Texas Christian University—pilfered 12 steals against Arkansas Pine Bluff. Daniels led the nation in the 2000–01 season with 108 steals and an average of 4.32 per game.

5. ALVIN ROBERTSON

Alvin Robertson made a career out of stealing the ball from his opponents. He remains the all-time NBA leader in steals per game with an amazing 2.71. He had 2,112 steals in 779 career games. In the 1985–86 season, he had 301 steals and an average of 3.67 per game for an NBA record, and in six separate seasons, he had at least 200 steals.

6. MICHAEL RAY RICHARDSON

The talented Michael Ray Richardson nabbed 1,463 steals in only 556 games, for an average of 2.63 per game. Richardson led the league in total steals four times in his short career.

7. JOHN STOCKTON

John Stockton retired in 2003 as the NBA's all-time leader in career steals with 3,265. During the course of his long career, he led the NBA in total steals twice, and had more than 200 steals for five consecutive seasons.

8. MICHAEL JORDAN

Michael Jordan is second of all-time in career steals with 2,514. In three separate seasons he was the NBA leader in total steals, and had six seasons with at least 200 steals.

9. DON BUSE

Don Buse was a tough 6′ 4″ guard who played for the Indiana Pacers, the Phoenix Suns, and the Portland Trailblazers. In his prime, Buse played for the Pacers in both the ABA and NBA. In the 1975–76 season, Buse grabbed an amazing 346 steals. In the Pacers' first year in the NBA (1976–77), Buse led his new league in steals with 281.

10. TED McCLAIN

On December 26, 1973, McClain—while a member of the Carolina Cougars—nabbed a record 12 steals in a single game against the New York Nets. The 12 steals were the all-time record for the ABA, and he led the ABA in steals with 250 during the 1973–74 season.

Terrific Trios

One player cannot win an NCAA or NBA championship. The great Oscar Robertson did not win an NBA title until he was a teammate of Kareem Abdul-Jabbar. The incomparable Michael Jordan did not win his first NBA title until his younger teammates Scottie Pippen and Horace Grant developed their skills. It has often been said that a team needs at least a three-pronged attack to be great, and these famous trios proved it.

1. BOSTON'S BIG THREE: LARRY BIRD, KEVIN McHALE, AND ROBERT PARISH

The Boston Celtics of the 1980s were a dominant force, battling the Los Angeles Lakers for NBA supremacy. The Celtics relied on an imposing front line called the "Big Three," which consisted of small forward Larry Bird, power forward Kevin McHale, and center Robert Parish. Bird provided great offense and solid rebounding. He was the NBA's MVP for three straight years from 1984–86. McHale possessed some of the finest post moves in the game. His long arms and great footwork confounded defenses. Robert Parish, affectionately called "Chief," did the dirty work in the paint and was one of the league's top centers.

2. THE TRIPLETS

The University of Arkansas Razorbacks made the NCAA Final Four in 1978 on the backs of three 6′ 4″ players, Sidney Moncrief, Ron Brewer, and Marvin Delph. They were dubbed "The Triplets" for their similar height and build by the great Al McGuire. All three averaged more than 16 points a game. Moncrief later earned fame in the NBA as an All-Star with the Milwaukee Bucks. Brewer also starred in the NBA, playing eight years for seven different teams. In the 1981–82 season with the Cleveland Cavaliers, he averaged nearly 19 points a game. Delph was a deadly outside shooter who, upon his graduation in 1978, left as Arkansas's all-time leading scorer (Moncrief passed him the next year). He never played in the NBA.

3. LETHAL WEAPON III

Georgia Tech reached the Final Four in 1990 because of its high scoring trio of point guard Kenny Anderson, off-guard Brian Oliver, and small forward Dennis Scott. Nicknamed "Lethal Weapon III" because of their potent offensive attack, the trio all averaged more than 20 points per game during the regular season. The Jackets lost to eventual champion UNLV Running Rebels in the semifinals 90–81. All three members of Lethal Weapon III played in the NBA after leaving Georgia Tech.

4. GAIL GOODRICH, JERRY WEST, AND WILT CHAMBERLAIN

The 1971–72 Los Angeles Lakers dominated the NBA, with a then-record 69 wins during the regular season.

They also won a record 33 consecutive games. The Lakers defeated the defending champion New York Knicks 4–1 in the finals, led by their high-scoring guards, Gail Goodrich and Jerry West, and their dominant force in the middle, Wilt Chamberlain. Goodrich averaged 25.9 points per game, while West averaged 25.8. Chamberlain averaged only 14.8 points per game, but he led the NBA in rebounding (19.2 per game) and field goal percentage. Many still consider the 1972 Lakers the greatest single-season team in the history of the NBA.

5. MICHAEL JORDAN, SCOTTIE PIPPEN, AND DENNIS RODMAN

For three straight years from 1996–98, the Chicago Bulls captured the NBA championship with a terrific trio. It consisted of the incomparable Michael Jordan, the versatile Scottie Pippen, and the rebounding machine Dennis Rodman. The trio led the Bulls to an NBA-best 72 wins in the 1995–96 regular season.

6. RUN TMC: TIM HARDAWAY, MITCH RICHMOND AND CHRIS MULLIN

The Golden State Warriors of the early 1990s featured the explosive "Run TMC"—a clear play on words from the pioneering rap group Run DMC. The Warriors featured point guard Tim Hardaway—with a devastating crossover dribble—shooting guard Mitch Richmond, and small forward Chris Mullin. In the 1990–91 season, Mullin averaged 25.7 points per game, Richmond 23.9 per game, and Hardaway 22.9.

7. GEORGE MIKAN, VERN MIKKELSEN, AND JIM POLLARD

The Minneapolis Lakers dominated the NBA in its early days, winning world titles in 1950, 1952, 1953, and

1954. The Lakers achieved success largely because of its imposing front line—6′ 10″ center George Mikan, 6′ 7″ power forward Vern Mikkelsen, and 6′ 5″ small forward Jim Pollard. All three were inducted into the Basketball Hall of Fame and appeared in multiple All-Star games.

8. ALEX ENGLISH, KIKI VANDEWEGHE, AND DAN ISSEL

The Denver Nuggets of the early 1980s were the highest scoring team in the NBA. During the 1981–82 season, the Nuggets averaged more than 126 points a game. Most of those points came from the trio of Alex English, Kiki Vandeweghe, and Dan Issel. The Nuggets' big three all averaged more than 20 points per game each for multiple years. In 1982–83, English and Vandeweghe finished in first and second place in scoring for the entire league. It was the first time that teammates had finished back-to-back in the scoring race since the 1954–55 season.

9. DALE ELLIS, TOM CHAMBERS, AND XAVIER MCDANIEL

The Seattle Supersonics of the mid- to late-1980s featured a potent offensive combination of sharpshooting guard Dale Ellis and forwards Tom Chambers and Xavier McDaniel. In the 1986–87 season, all three averaged at least 23 points per game. They were the first trio in NBA history to have three players average that many points per game.

10. THE THREE J'S

Not all trios live up to their talent. Such was the case for the Dallas Mavericks' young triumvirate of point guard

Jason Kidd, shooting guard Jimmy Jackson, and small forward Jamal Mashburn. The Mavericks thought that the addition of lottery draft picks Jackson (1992), Kidd (1993) and Mashburn (1994) would lead the team to the upper echelon of the NBA. It did not work out that way, because egos clashed between the young stars. All three players were traded by 1996. "We were young," Jamal Mashburn told ace NBA writer David Aldridge for his April 2005 story for ESPN.com, "and everybody wanted the limelight just a little bit too early."

Sixth Men

J ohn Starks, who won an NBA Sixth Man of the Year Award, once said: "It's not how much time you're in the game, it's what you do with that time." During the 2003–04 season, Antawn Jamison came off the Dallas Mavericks' bench for the first time in his career. Formerly, Jamison was a high-scoring forward for the Golden State Warriors. He sacrificed his playing time in Dallas for the benefit of the team and was rewarded with the Sixth Man of the Year award. These ten players were ideal Sixth Men, providing their teams with an instant spark off the bench.

1. FRANK RAMSEY

Frank Ramsey became the first great Sixth Man in the 1955–56 when Boston Celtics' legendary coach Arnold "Red" Auerbach brought him off the bench to provide extra scoring punch.

2. JOHN HAVLICEK

John Havlicek became the Celtics' second super Sixth Man, replacing the great Frank Ramsey. For his first six seasons, Havlicek came off the bench to spark his team. Havlicek made the All-Star team thirteen times and played a total of sixteen seasons. He scored more than 26,000 points in his career.

3. KEVIN McHALE

Kevin McHale became one of the NBA's all-time greatest power forwards. Charles Barkley often called him the toughest player he ever had to guard. When McHale came to the Celtics as a rookie in 1980, the Celtics' power forward was Cedric "Cornbread" Maxwell. McHale came off the bench for the first four years of his career. He excelled in the Sixth Man role, capturing Sixth Man of the Year Awards in 1984 and 1985.

4. BOBBY JONES

Bobby Jones of the Philadelphia 76ers excelled as a Sixth Man. The NBA began awarding the Sixth Man of the Year Award in 1983, and for his efforts off the bench, Jones captured the inaugural award. Jones was known as one of the game's premier defensive players, and he made the league's All-Defensive First Team several times.

5. RICKY PIERCE

Ricky Pierce played fifteen years in the NBA for several teams. During his prime, he starred for the Milwaukee Bucks and captured two Sixth Man of the Year Awards in 1987 and 1990. Pierce was known for his deadly mid-range jumper and his strong upper body, which enabled him to drive effectively to the hoop.

6. DETLEF SCHREMPF

Detlef Schrempf was a versatile 6' 10" forward from Germany who played collegiately at the University of

Washington. Drafted by Dallas, Schrempf played there for several years before going to the Indiana Pacers. As a Pacer, Schrempf created a niche for himself as an ideal Sixth Man. He embodied the role so much that he won back-to-back Sixth Man of the Year Awards in 1991 and 1992. Schrempf later started for the Seattle Supersonics and was named to three All-Star games in his career.

7. VINNIE JOHNSON

Vinnie "The Microwave" Johnson never won a Sixth Man of the Year Award during his great career with the Detroit Pistons, but he was a dynamite Sixth Man coming off the bench to supply instant offense. Johnson's shot was unblockable, and when he got hot he could literally take over a game. He played a key role on the Pistons' championship teams of 1989–90 and 1990–91.

8. DELL CURRY

Dell Curry was not a great rebounder, defender, or passer. He was in the league for primarily one reason—his shooting. Curry had great range, a super-quick release, and confidence. His performance during the 1993–94 season—he averaged 16.3 points per game off the bench—earned him the NBA's Sixth Man of the Year Award.

9. JOHN WILLIAMS

John "Hot Rod" Williams starred for the Cleveland Cavaliers as a back-up power forward and center. Williams often played behind center Brad Daugherty and power forward Larry Nance, but he played great as a

Sixth Man, averaging double figures and contributing mightily in rebounds and blocked shots.

10. TONI KUKOC

Croatia's Toni Kukoc starred on three championship teams for the Chicago Bulls from 1996–1998. Kukoc did not start because Scottie Pippen and Dennis Rodman were the regular forwards. However, Kukoc played a key role for the Bulls with his shooting, ball-handling and great passing. He is called "The Server" for his ability to serve up teammates with easy buckets. In 2004–05, Kukoc still served up assists for his teammates on the Milwaukee Bucks.

She Can Hoop, Too

Basketball is no longer just a guy's game. One need only see the popularity of college and professional women's basketball to acknowledge that females can play ball. As with other sports, athletic genes seem to run in the family. These ten female b-ballers have male relatives who could also play a little basketball.

1. **CHERYL MILLER**

Cheryl Miller is considered by some experts to be the greatest women's basketball player of all time. She was an All-American all four years at the University of Southern California, and was named the national Player of the Year her last three years there. She scored more than 3,000 points in her illustrious college career and won a gold medal at the 1984 Olympics. She coached two years at USC and then coached several years in the WNBA with the Phoenix Mercury. She is now a commentator for NBA games.

Despite all of her many accomplishments, many only know Cheryl as the sister of Indiana Pacer great Reggie Miller.

2. CHERYL FORD

Cheryl Ford has established herself as one of the top young stars of the WNBA, and she helped lead the Detroit Shock to their first championship in 2003. For her efforts, Ford was a near unanimous selection as the WNBA's Rookie of the Year. Cheryl's father is none other than NBA great Karl Malone. Ford followed in her father's footsteps by playing college ball at Louisiana Tech. She was twice the conference Player of the Year in college.

3. DEBRA RODMAN

Before Dennis "The Worm" Rodman gained fame with his rebounding skills as a Detroit Piston, his sister Debra carried the family name quite well under the boards. Debra Rodman played for Louisiana Tech in the early 1980s. In the 1982–83 season, Debra led the Lady Techsters with 10.7 rebounds per game. She helped carry her team to the national championship game, where they lost to a Cheryl Miller–led USC squad 69–67. In the 1983–84 season, Debra again led her team in rebounding. Debra and Dennis's sister Kim Rodman also starred in college basketball at Stephen F. Austin State University.

4. TAMIKA CATCHINGS

Tamika Catchings is an All-Star forward with the WNBA's Indiana Fever. She made the league's All-WNBA team in 2002 and 2003. In 2003, she was runner-up for both the MVP and Defensive Player of the Year Awards. In 2004, Tamika won the MVP award. She played collegiately at the University of Tennessee, where she was part of two NCAA tournament championships.

Tamika and her twin sister Tauja got their basketball bloodlines from their father, former NBA player Harvey Catchings. Harvey played in the league from 1973 until 1985. Known as a defensive stopper and shotblocker, he played for the Philadelphia 76ers, Milwaukee Bucks, New Jersey Nets, and the Los Angeles Clippers.

5. KHARA SMITH

Khara Smith, along with her cousin Charlene, is a star player for the DePaul Blue Demons' women's basketball team. Smith earned Freshman of the Year honors in Conference USA in her freshman season. She averaged more than 20 points per game and nearly 12 rebounds per game as a sophomore. She was named an honorable mention All-American in 2003–04. Smith's father is Ken Norman, a former All-America basketball player at the University of Illinois. Norman played for the Illini from 1983–1987. He played eight years in the NBA, including time with the Los Angeles Clippers, Milwaukee Bucks, and Atlanta Hawks.

6. NATALIE WILLIAMS

Natalie Williams is one of the top players in women's professional basketball. She is a three-time All-Star selection and led the WNBA in rebounding in 2000 with 11.6 rebounds per game. Williams began her WNBA career with the Utah Starzz and then moved to the Indiana Fever. She played collegiately at UCLA, where she was an All-American in both basketball and volleyball. Her father, Nate Williams, played eight seasons in the NBA with the Cincinnati Royals, the Kansas City Kings, the New Orleans Jazz, and the Golden State Warriors.

7. **KANDYCE GREEN**

Kandyce Green is a star guard for Lake Forrest College in Chicago. As a freshman, Green scored 25 points in one game and led her team in scoring at nearly 12 points per game. In 2003–04, she averaged more than 13 points per game and earned First-Team All-Conference honors. Kandyce is the daughter of former NBA point guard Rickey Green, who starred for the Utah Jazz and Charlotte Hornets.

8. **STACEYANN CLAXTON**

The basketball programs at Hofstra University owe a large debt of gratitude to the Claxton family. That's because Staceyann Claxton and her brother Craig "Speedy" Claxton were starting point guards for their respective teams at Hofstra. Staceyann played from 2000–04, leading her team in assists and steals. Speedy played at Hofstra from 1996–2000, scoring more than 2,000 points in his stellar career. Speedy has moved on to the NBA, logging time with the Philadelphia 76ers, San Antonio Spurs, and Golden State Warriors. He was part of San Antonio's championship squad in 2002–03.

But Speedy is not the only star in the family. As Staceyann's college coach said of her: "She has certainly made a name for herself."

9. **MFON UDOKA**

Mfon Udoka played basketball for the WNBA's Houston Comets. Prior to that, she played with the Detroit Shock. She played collegiately at DePaul University where she scored more than 1,500 points in her career.

Mfon, along with her brother Ime, became the first brother-sister duo in the WNBA and the NBA. Ime, who played collegiately at Portland State, played a few games in the 2003–04 season with the Los Angeles Lakers.

10. **MARGARET RIAK DeCIMAN**

Margaret Riak DeCiman stands 6′ 7″, and she dominated junior college basketball with her blocking at Seward County Community College in Kansas. In February 2004 she announced that she would play for Louisiana Tech University. DeCiman's uncle is none other than Manute Bol, the 7′ 7″ center who played ten years in the NBA, leading the league his first year in blocked shots with nearly 5 per game. He played with the Washington Bullets, Philadelphia 76ers, Golden State Warriors, and Miami Heat during his career.

Unlikely NBA and ABA Record Holders

M any of the NBA's and ABA's greatest records have been set by players that would surprise both the casual and expert fan alike. These unlikely players have their names etched in NBA and ABA history for some impressive records.

1. SCOTT SKILES

When thinking of assists, one thinks of Earvin "Magic" Johnson, Bob Cousy, or the all-time leader, John Stockton. One certainly doesn't think of Scott Skiles, the head coach of the Chicago Bulls. Skiles played for five teams in ten years, and his highest season assist average was 8.4. However, on December 30, 1990, Skiles dished out 30 assists to lead the Orlando Magic to a 155–116 win over the Denver Nuggets. Bryan Burrell puts it best in *At The Buzzer: The Greatest Moments in NBA History*: "Out of all the point guards in NBA history, the idea that Scott Skiles would become the record holder for most assists in a game is as unlikely as a house painter ending up in the Louvre."

2. JERRY HARKNESS

Jerry Harkness made one three-pointer during the inaugural ABA season of 1966–67, but that one shot has landed him in the annals of basketball folklore. On November 13, 1967, the Dallas Chapparels held a 118–116 lead over Harkness's Indiana Pacers with only 1 second remaining. The Pacers inbounded the ball to Harkness who threw up a 92-foot hook shot. Amazingly, the ball banked in off the glass and the Pacers won by a single point. As Harkness says in Terry Pluto's entertaining book about the ABA, *Loose Balls*: "The irony is that I wasn't much of an outside shooter. In fact, that was the only three-pointer I made that season."

3. SLEEPY FLOYD

In the May 1987 playoff series between the powerful Los Angeles Lakers and the upstart Golden State Warriors, the Lakers were ahead 2–0 and well on their way to a three-game sweep. However, in the second half, Warriors' guard Eric "Sleepy" Floyd awoke in a major way. He erupted for 29 points in the final quarter and 51 for the game. Floyd's 29 points were the most ever scored by an NBA player in one quarter in a playoff game. Floyd never averaged more than 20 points per game in a single NBA season, but he gave the NBA one of its greatest single-game individual performances.

4. BOB HANSEN

Bobby Hansen was a career 32.3% three-point shooter in his ten-year NBA career. He never led the league in any shooting category during his entire career. But for some reason, Hansen had the three-point stroke during the playoffs. In the 1987–88 playoffs with the Utah

Jazz, Hansen shot 19 out of 36. For his career, Hansen sank 38 of 76 three-point shots in the playoffs for an impressive 50%.

5. JAMES DONALDSON

James Donaldson was a hulking 7' 2" center who played for five teams in his fourteen-year career. He led the league in field-goal percentage in the 1984–85 season while he was a member of the Los Angeles Clippers. It may come as some surprise, however, that Donaldson is the NBA's all-time field goal percentage leader in playoff history. Donaldson made 153 out of 244 shots for 62.7%. The next highest playoff total is by Kurt Rambis at 57.4%.

6. LARRY KENON and KENDALL GILL

Neither Larry Kenon nor Kendall Gill rank among the NBA's top 30 players in steals per game in their career. Kenon never led the league in steals in any season of his career from 1973–1983. However, Larry "Special K" Kenon nabbed 11 steals in a December 26, 1976 game against the Kansas City Kings while he was a member of the San Antonio Spurs. The record still stands in the NBA, though Gill matched it in a 1999 game against the Miami Heat, while he was a member of the New Jersey Nets.

7. CHARLIE SCOTT

The wide-open ABA featured some of professional basketball's greatest scorers. Among them were Rick Barry, George Gervin, Julius Erving, Dan Issel, and Spencer Haywood. But the highest scoring average in the history of the ABA belonged to Charlie Scott. In his second season with the Virginia Squires in 1971–72, Scott averaged 34.6 points per game. Scott's next highest season scoring average was during his first year in the ABA at 27.1 points per game.

8. NATE THURMOND

Nate Thurmond was a bruising 6′ 11″ Hall of Fame center who played with several teams from 1963–1977 in the NBA. He was often overshadowed by other more dominant centers, such as Wilt Chamberlain, Bill Russell, and Kareem Abdul-Jabbar. But on the opening night of the 1974 season, Thurmond recorded the first quadruple double (double figures in four categories) in NBA history with 22 points, 14 rebounds, 13 assists and 12 blocked shots.

9. KOBE BRYANT

Kobe Bryant has never been considered one of the NBA's best three-point shooters. In two of his seasons, he shot under 30% from outside. On January 7, 2003, Bryant unleashed perhaps the greatest single-game shooting performance in NBA history when he drained 12 threes against the Seattle Supersonics. His amazing performance included nine straight three-pointers without a miss. His then-coach Phil Jackson called it the greatest shooting streak he'd ever seen. Opposing coach Nate McMillan said: "'I don't think most guys can do that in a gym by themselves, let alone a game where you're being defended."

10. MICHEAL WILLIAMS

Micheal Williams never led the NBA in free-throw percentage in any season in his career. In his rookie season, he shot only 66% from the charity stripe. However, from March to November of 1993, during the course of two seasons, Williams was automatic. He made an NBA record 97 consecutive free throws. The next highest total is 81 by Mahmoud Abdul-Rauf.

Undrafted Stars

M ost players enter the NBA via the draft held each June. Originally consisting of as many as ten rounds, the draft is now only two rounds, where teams get to choose their next potential star. The following ten players did not follow the traditional route; instead, they made an NBA squad the hard way.

1. BEN WALLACE

Ben Wallace was not drafted in 1996 after playing college ball at Virginia Union. He did make the roster of the Washington Bullets, but he played very little during his first season. Eventually, Wallace proved that all the teams in the NBA made a mistake of epic proportions in passing him up. Wallace led the NBA in rebounding in the 2001–02 and 2002–03 seasons. He also earned Defensive Player of the Year during that time. In 2003–04, Wallace anchored the Pistons' defense, which carried them to an NBA championship.

2. AVERY JOHNSON

Avery Johnson led the NCAA in assists during his last two seasons at Southern University. His senior year in

1987–88, he averaged an amazing 13.3 assists per game. However, he was not selected in the 1988 NBA draft. Johnson played with the United States Basketball League's (USBL) Palm Beach Stingrays before making the Seattle Supersonics' roster. He has played in the NBA ever since. At the peak of his career, he was the starting point guard and team leader for the San Antonio Spurs. He hit the series-winning shot with 2.5 seconds remaining in Game 5 of the 1999 championship to lead his Spurs over the New York Knicks 4–1. He now coaches the Dallas Mavericks.

3. **DARRELL ARMSTRONG**

Darrell Armstrong was not drafted after completing his college career at Fayetteville State in 1991. Armstrong played in the Global Basketball League, the USBL, the CBA, Greece, and Spain before finally landing with the Orlando Magic in 1995. His energetic play earned him the respect of the entire league, and he averaged double figures off the bench for four straight years.

4. **BRAD MILLER**

Despite a stellar career at Purdue University, no NBA team picked 6′ 11″ Brad Miller in the 1998 NBA draft. Instead, Miller took his game to Italy, and eventually landed on the Charlotte Hornets in 1999. He continued on to the Chicago Bulls and then the Indiana Pacers. Miller made his first All-Star appearance with the Pacers in the 2002–03 season. Traded to the Sacramento Kings, Miller played even better, earning his second straight All-Star game appearance. He averaged 14 points and 10 rebounds per game for the Kings.

5. **JOHN STARKS**

John Starks played collegiately at Oklahoma State, but was not picked in the 1988 NBA draft. He played in 36 games with the Golden State Warriors in the 1988–89 season. Even so, Starks still had to play in the CBA and the World Basketball League (WBL) for much of 1989 and 1990. He landed in the NBA again with the New York Knicks for the 1990–91 season, and he played eight years with them. In 1993–94, he averaged 19 points per game and helped lead the Knicks to the brink of an NBA title, before falling to the Houston Rockets in a hotly contested seven-game series. In 1996–97, Starks was the NBA's Sixth Man of the Year.

6. BO OUTLAW

Charles "Bo" Outlaw was not drafted in 1993, even after an outstanding career at the University of Houston. Instead, Outlaw played in Spain and the CBA before landing with the Los Angeles Clippers. A high-energy, hustle player, Outlaw creates havoc on the floor with his relentless pursuit of the basketball and opposing players. His hustle has earned him a place in the NBA for more than a dozen seasons.

7. ROBERT PACK

The super-quick Robert Pack was not drafted after his college career at the University of Southern California. Pack landed as a free agent with the Portland Trailblazers and has remained in the league since. In 31 games with the Washington Bullets in 1995–96, Pack averaged more than 18 points per game, once scoring 35 points in one game.

8. MARQUIS DANIELS

Despite leading Auburn University to the Sweet Sixteen in the 2003 NCAA tournament, no NBA team drafted Marquis Daniels. However, the 6′ 6″ versatile rookie

made the Dallas Mavericks as an undrafted free agent.
He averaged 8.5 points per game off the bench for the
high-octane Mavs in the 2003–04 season. Then, in the
playoff series versus the Sacramento Kings, Daniels
averaged more than 15 points per game. The Mavericks' coach Don Nelson said that Marquis was one of
the best rookies he has ever coached.

9. BRUCE BOWEN

Bruce Bowen was not drafted by any NBA, or even any
CBA, team after a four-year career at Cal State Fuller-
ton. Bowen played overseas in France for several
teams, and one year in the CBA. He finally latched on
with the Miami Heat at the end of the 1996–97 season.
He took his career to another level with the San Antonio
Spurs, and led the NBA in three-point field goal percentage in the 2002–03 season. However, Bowen is
primarily known as a defensive stopper. He won the
NBA's Defensive Player of the Year award in 2003–04.

10. EARL BOYKINS

Earl Boykins was not drafted despite a stellar career at
Eastern Michigan University. Many scouts were likely
leery of his 5' 5" frame, but they underestimated Boykins's giant heart and amazing skills. Though he has
bounced around to seven teams in eight years, Boykins
seems to have found a home with the Denver Nuggets.
In the 2003–04 and 2004–05 seasons, Boykins averaged double figures off the bench. He frequently sparks
the team and remains on the floor in the fourth quarter
when the game is on the line. In the first round of the
2004–05 NBA playoffs, Boykins scored 32 points in
one game against the San Antonio Spurs.

Terrible Trades

I n the summer of 2004, the Los Angeles Lakers made a monumental decision to trade their franchise center Shaquille O'Neal to the Miami Heat for Lamar Odom, Brian Grant, and Caron Butler. Time will tell if this was a terrible trade for either the Lakers or the Heat. However, the following ten trades were among the most lopsided in NBA history.

1. EARL MONROE FOR MIKE RIORDAN AND DAVE STALLWORTH

In November 1971, the Baltimore Bullets traded their star player Earl "The Pearl" Monroe to the New York Knicks for Mike Riordan and Dave Stallworth. The trade paid immediate dividends for the Knicks, who placed Monroe in the backcourt with his former rival Walt "Clyde" Frazier. Frazier and Monroe led the Knicks to the 1972 NBA Finals where they lost to the Lakers. Then, Monroe helped lead the Knicks to the 1973 title, defeating the Lakers 4–1 in a Finals rematch. Riordan had two decent years with Baltimore before moving to Washington with the Bullets. Stall-worth only averaged 6 points per game for Baltimore.

2. ROBERT PARISH AND A DRAFT PICK FOR TWO DRAFT PICKS

In June 1980, Celtics general manager Arnold "Red" Auerbach pulled off one of the best trades in NBA his-tory. The Celtics traded away the number one and number 13 upcoming draft picks to the Golden State Warriors for center Robert Parish and the number three pick in the draft. The Warriors used their two draft picks to select center Joe Barry Carroll and power forward Rickey Brown. Carroll actually had some fine years in the NBA, averaging more than 24 points one season. However, Brown proved relatively ineffective. The Celt-ics, on the other hand, used their number three draft pick to select Kevin McHale. McHale and Parish be-came All-Stars and Hall of Famers. Along with Larry Bird, they formed perhaps the greatest frontcourt in NBA history.

3. WILT CHAMBERLAIN FOR THREE PLAYERS AND CASH

On January 15, 1965, the San Fransisco Warriors traded the great Wilt Chamberlain to the Philadelphia 76ers for Connie Dierking, Paul Neumann, Lee Shaffer, and cash. They plummeted to a record of 17–63 after trading Chamberlain, who had led the league in scoring the previous six years. Chamberlain led the 76ers to an NBA title in his second full season in 1968. Meanwhile, the Warriors profited little from the three players it picked up in the infamous trade.

Harlem Globetrotters

Wilt Chamberlain with the Harlem Globetrotters.

4. DIRK NOWITZKI AND PAT GARRITY FOR ROBERT TRAYLOR

Don Nelson, the coach and general manager for the Dallas Mavericks, made one of the greatest trades in NBA history when he convinced the Milwaukee Bucks—the team that Nelson coached for many years—to trade Dirk Nowitzki and Pat Garrity for power forward Robert "Tractor" Traylor. The deal called for Dallas to select Traylor with its number six pick in the draft. The Bucks would select Nowitzki at number nine and Garrity at number 19. The trade turned out to be very lopsided; Traylor never developed into a star player for the Bucks, or anywhere else, and Nowitzki has become one of the NBA's best players. For example, in the 2004–05 season, Nowitzki averaged 26 points per game for Dallas. Traylor averaged 5.5 for Cleveland. Nelson later said that "drafting Tractor Traylor looks good on my trade resume." That was quite an understatement.

5. VINNIE JOHNSON FOR GREG KELSER

In November 1981, the Seattle Supersonics traded guard Vinnie Johnson to the Detroit Pistons for Greg "Special K" Kelser. Kelser was the better known of the two players, as he had teamed up with Magic Johnson to win the NCAA title in 1979 for Michigan State. Meanwhile, Vinnie Johnson had labored in relative obscurity at Baylor. However, the trade might have been his big chance. Kelser never produced in Seattle or for the rest of his NBA career. Johnson, meanwhile, became a mainstay of instant offense for the Pistons off the bench. Known as "The Microwave" for his ability to heat up on his shooting, Johnson became a key ingredient on the Pistons' back-to-back NBA championship teams.

6. BERNARD KING FOR MICHAEL RAY RICHARDSON

On October 22, 1982, the Golden State Warriors traded forward Bernard King to the New York Knicks for the talented but troubled guard Michael Ray Richardson and a fifth-round draft pick. At the time, the trade seemed somewhat balanced, as both King and Richardson had battled substance abuse issues. However, King resurrected his career with the New York Knicks, leading the NBA in scoring. Richardson was another story. He lasted only 33 games with the Warriors before being traded to the New Jersey Nets, and he was eventually kicked out of the NBA for repeated positive drug tests.

7. RICK MAHORN FOR DAN ROUNDFIELD

This was bad news for the Bullets and another great trade for the Detroit Pistons. In June 1985, the Pistons unloaded power forward Dan Roundfield for the Washington Bullets' power forward Rick Mahorn. Roundfield had been an All-Star power forward for many years for the Atlanta Hawks, but he did not perform well as a Piston. Roundfield didn't play well in Washington either, and his best years were clearly behind him. Mahorn helped turn the Pistons into the "Bad Boys," making them into the toughest and meanest team in the league. Mahorn, as a starting power forward, played a key role on the Pistons' first championship team of 1988–89.

8. KAREEM ABDUL-JABBAR FOR FOUR LAKERS

In June 1975, the Milwaukee Bucks traded their great center Kareem Abdul-Jabbar and Walt Wesley to the

Los Angeles Lakers for Elmore Smith, Junior Bridgeman, Brian Winters, and Dave Meyers. The trade proved momentous for the Lakers, as Kareem later led the Lakers to five NBA championships with the help of Earvin "Magic" Johnson. The Bucks acquired some decent players in Bridgeman and Winters, but they were not Hall of Fame material. Simply stated, the trade led to five NBA championships for the Lakers and not one for the Bucks.

9. ELVIN HAYES FOR JACK MARIN

In June 1972, the Houston Rockets traded Elvin Hayes to the Baltimore Bullets for Jack Marin and future considerations. The trade was one of the most lopsided in NBA history. Hayes turned in numerous All-Star seasons for the Bullets, while Marin's production plummeted. Hayes helped lead the Bullets to three NBA Finals appearances and a championship in 1978. He retired with more than 27,000 career points.

10. CHARLES BARKLEY FOR JEFF HORNACEK, TIM PERRY, AND ANDREW LANG

In June 1992, the Philadelphia 76ers traded the talented Charles Barkley to the Phoenix Suns for three players—sharpshooting guard Jeff Hornacek, forward Tim Perry, and center Andrew Lang. The trade paid immediate dividends for the Suns, as "Sir Charles" led the Suns to a 63-win season and a berth in the NBA Finals against the Chicago Bulls. The 76ers, on the other hand, struggled after the trade. Hornacek performed well but lasted only two years with the 76ers before moving to Utah. Perry was a disappointment, averaging only nine points a game. Lang only played one year for the 76ers and was never really a factor.

Clipping Talents

The Los Angeles (formerly San Diego) Clippers have been in the lower echelon of the NBA for a long time. The team has had some good talent in its history, but somehow manages to miss the playoffs nearly every year. One problem is that the Clippers have made some horrible draft selections. Another problem has been a failure to hold on to talent. Here are ten examples of Clipper catastrophes.

1. TERRY CUMMINGS

In 1984, the San Diego Clippers traded their best player, Terry Cummings, in a multi-player deal to the Milwaukee Bucks. The best player they received in return was former UCLA star Marques Johnson, who was five years older than Cummings. Cummings had averaged more than 23 points per game for the Clippers in his two seasons with the team. He went on to have a long career with the Milwaukee Bucks and the San Antonio Spurs. Johnson, on the other hand, had two decent seasons for the Clippers before injuries and age took their toll.

2. TOM CHAMBERS

The San Diego Clippers selected Tom Chambers with the number eight pick in the 1981 NBA draft. He played for two years before being traded to the Seattle Supersonics. Chambers blossomed into a superstar at Seattle and then at Phoenix, where he became a perennial 20-point-per-game scorer. The Clippers should never have let him go.

3. BYRON SCOTT

The San Diego Clippers selected guard Byron Scott of Arizona State as the fourth pick in the 1983 NBA draft. The Clippers then traded Scott to the Los Angeles Lakers for veteran guard Norm Nixon. Nixon was talented, but he was also injured often. Scott played ten years for the Lakers, most of them as the starting shooting guard on several championship teams. This was another bad play for the Clippers.

4. DANNY FERRY

Hindsight is 20/20, but the Clippers should have seen this coming. With the second pick in the 1989 NBA draft, they selected Danny Ferry out of Duke. Rather than play for the Clippers, Ferry went to Italy and played professional basketball there. He eventually began his NBA career in Cleveland. The Clippers passed on such talents as Glen Rice, Sean Elliott, Mookie Blaylock, and Tim Hardaway by using their number two pick on Danny Ferry.

5. LORENZEN WRIGHT

In the 1996 NBA draft, the Clippers drafted Lorenzen Wright out of Memphis State with the seventh pick in

the draft. Wright played three years for the Clippers before moving to Atlanta and Memphis. Wright actually
has developed into a good player for Memphis, but the
Clippers could have drafted Kobe Bryant. Instead, the
crosstown Lakers selected Bryant with the thirteenth
pick, and the rest is history.

6. BENOIT BENJAMIN

In the 1985 NBA draft, the Los Angeles Clippers saw
potential in Creighton University's giant center Benoit
Benjamin. They selected Benjamin with the third pick
in the draft. They passed on many players who were
much better, however. For example, Utah selected Karl
Malone with the thirteenth pick, Seattle selected Xavier
McDaniel with the fourth pick, and the Los Angeles
Lakers selected A.C. Green with the twenty-third pick.
Benjamin had his moments but he never lived up to his
potential—or his high draft selection.

7. MICHAEL OLOWAKANDI

This might have been the dumbest draft decision the
Clippers have ever made, and that is saying a lot. In the
1998 NBA draft, the Clippers had the first overall pick
in the draft and used it to select center Michael Olowakandi out of Pacific. Olowakandi has a nice jump hook
but has never blossomed into a star. He is now a reserve for the Minnesota Timberwolves. Players the
Clippers passed on include stars such as Mike Bibby,
Antawn Jamison, Vince Carter, and Dirk Nowitzki.

8. WILCOX OVER STOUDAMIRE

In the 2002 NBA draft the Los Angeles Clippers used
their number eight pick to select Chris Wilcox, who entered the pro ranks early from the University of Maryland.

Wilcox has yet to develop into a consistent player or even a starter. With the very next pick, the Phoenix Suns selected Amare Stoudamire out of high school. Stoudamire is a legitimate star in the league, and was averaging 26 points per game in 2004–05.

9. DEHERE OVER CASSELL

In the 1993 NBA draft, the Los Angeles Clippers had an unlucky number thirteen draft pick. The position proved to be fitting as they chose Terry Dehere from Seton Hall who had a fine college career. However, Dehere never materialized in the NBA. The Clippers could have chosen Florida State's guard Sam Cassell who ended up the number twenty-four pick for the Houston Rockets. Cassell played a key role in the Rockets' back-to-back NBA titles in 1994 and 1995.

10. CRAIG HODGES

The San Diego Clippers selected Craig Hodges out of Long Beach State in the third round of the 1982 NBA draft. However, Hodges played only two years with the Clippers before being shipped to Milwaukee. Hodges, a deadly three-point shooter, later was a reserve on several Chicago Bulls championship teams.

Sultans of Swat

The last line of defense often resides with a shot-blocking center or forward. Certain players have been able to change games with their defensive presence and shot blocking. These skills have also led to some intriguing nicknames. For example Marvin Webster was known as the "Human Eraser" for his shot blocking ability. These players deserve to be called the Sultans of Swat.

1. ELMORE SMITH

Elmore Smith was a seven-footer out of Kentucky State University. Drafted by the Buffalo Braves, Smith played two seasons with them before being traded to the Los Angeles Lakers in 1973. The 1973–74 season was the first time the NBA kept statistics for blocked shots. That year Smith led the league with 393 blocks in 81 games, for an average of 4.85. On October 28, 1973, Smith set an NBA record by blocking 17 shots in a game against the Portland Trailblazers. Smith's single-game record still stands.

2. KEITH CLOSS

Keith Closs was a slender 7′ 3″ center for Central Connecticut State in 1994–96. In his two years there, he led the NCAA in blocked shots. In his sophomore season in 1996, he blocked an astonishing 178 shots in 28 games, for an average of 6.36 per game. Closs later played three seasons for the Los Angeles Clippers from 1997 to 2000. Despite playing limited minutes in a total of 130 NBA games for his career, Closs blocked 163 shots.

3. DAVID ROBINSON

David Robinson, known as "The Admiral," led the NCAA in blocked shots his last two years at Navy. His junior year (1985–86), he led the nation with 207 blocks in 35 games, for an average of 5.91. His senior year (1986–87), he again led the country in blocks with 144 in 32 games, for an average of 4.5 per game. In the professional ranks, he blocked more than 300 shots in each of his first three seasons. He led the league in total blocks for the 1990–91 and 1991–92 seasons. His efforts during the 1991–92 season earned him Defensive Player of the Year honors. He retired with 2,954 blocks.

4. MARK EATON

Utah's hulking 7′ 4″ center Mark Eaton blocked more than 3,000 shots in his 11-year career with the Jazz. Eaton led the NBA in total blocks for four seasons. In the 1984–85 season, Eaton rejected an astonishing 456 blocks for an average of 5.56 per game.

5. MANUTE BOL

Manute Bol was a skinny 7′ 6″ center who played collegiately at Bridgeport. Bol began his NBA career in

1985 with the Washington Bullets. He led the NBA in blocked shots with 397 in 1985–86 and 345 in 1988–89.

6. HAKEEM OLAJUWON

Hakeem "The Dream" Olajuwon is one of the greatest centers in NBA history. He was perennially among the league's leaders in blocked shots. He led the league in blocks twice in his career, in the 1989–90 and 1992–93 seasons. When Olajuwon retired after the 2001–02 season, he held the all-time record for blocks with 3,830.

7. DIKEMBE MUTOMBO

The 7′ 2″ Dikembe Mutombo has been a defensive demon in the NBA for many years. After blocking an opponent's shot, Mutombo taunts his opponents by wagging his finger back and forth. He led the NBA in total number of blocked shots for five straight seasons from 1992–93 through the 1997–98 season.

8. ADONAL FOYLE

Adonal Foyle blocked 492 shots during his three-year college career at Colgate, from 1995–1997. In his junior season, Foyle swatted 180 shots in 28 games for an amazing average of 6.43 per game. Though not a starter, Foyle continues to block shots in the professional ranks with the Golden State Warriors. For example, during the 2002–03 season, he blocked 205 shots.

9. BILL RUSSELL

Bill Russell was the legendary Celtics center who led his team to 11 NBA titles in thirteen seasons. Though the league didn't keep blocked shot statistics during his career, many believe that he dominated the category. Russell not only blocked shots, but he swatted them to his teammates to start fast breaks. He is widely considered to be the greatest defensive player in NBA history.

10. THEO RATLIFF

Theo Ratliff is a 6' 10" leaper out of the University of Wyoming. In his final year of college in 1995 he blocked 144 shots in 28 games, for an average of 5.14 per game. He led the NBA in blocked shots in both the 2002–03 and 2003–04 seasons, and he has already blocked more than 1,700 shots in his NBA career.

Not a Scorer

M ost basketball players like to shoot the ball and score points because that is what generally draws attention, acclaim, and applause. However, other players realize that their role is defined in other areas, such as good defense or rebounding. The following ten professional players have all grabbed more total rebounds than points in their NBA careers.

1. NATE THURMOND

Hall of Fame center Nate Thurmond scored a respectable 14,437 points in fourteen NBA seasons. However, Thurmond's bread-and-butter skills were tough defense and rebounding. Thurmond grabbed a total of 14,464 rebounds in his career, and he led the NBA in rebounding during the 1969–70 season. Thurmond's career averages were remarkable—15 points and 15 rebounds per game. He played his first two seasons as power forward for the San Francisco Warriors alongside dominating center Wilt Chamberlain. Thurmond's development was a factor in the Warrior's decision to trade Chamberlain in 1965.

2. DENNIS RODMAN

Dennis Rodman was a 6′ 7″ rebounding fool of a forward who led the NBA in the category an amazing seven seasons in a row, from the 1991–92 season through the 1997–98 season. He collected nearly 12,000 rebounds in his career. By contrast, Rodman scored 6,683 points in his career. He averaged double figures in scoring only once in his entire career. Rodman was a lousy shooter who rarely took an outside shot. His free-throw percentage was terrible, but he may well have earned his ticket to the Hall of Fame with his exceptional rebounding. His excellence under the boards helped him lead two of his teams to a total of five NBA championships—two with the Detroit Pistons and three with the Chicago Bulls.

3. BEN WALLACE

"Big Ben" Wallace is the best rebounder in the NBA today, leading the league in rebounding in the 2001–02 and 2002–03 seasons. In the 2002–03 season, Wallace averaged 15.4 rebounds per contest—by far the best in the league. At the end of the 2003–04 season, Wallace had grabbed 5,654 rebounds. Meanwhile, Wallace has scored only 3,309 points. He definitely knows his role—defense and rebounding. Perhaps that is one reason why the Detroit Pistons won the 2004 NBA championship.

4. MANUTE BOL

Manute Bol was a razor-thin 7′ 6″ defensive presence whose primary role was to block shots. In his rookie season with the Washington Bullets in 1985–86, Bol tallied an amazing 397 blocked shots. In three separate seasons, he blocked 397 shots in 85–86, 302 shots in 86–87 and 345 shots in 88–89. By contrast, the greatest number of total points he scored in a single season was 314. Bol had few offensive skills, posting a career scoring average of 2.8 points per game. By contrast, Bol has a career rebounding average of 4.2. Bol also has more career blocked shots (2,086) than points (1,599).

5. MARK EATON

Mark Eaton was a 7′ 4″ defensive presence for the Utah Jazz from 1984–1993. Eaton had few offensive skills, but he led the league in blocked shots four times in his career. Eaton rarely ever shot from more than five feet from the basket, but he still managed only a 45.8% field goal average in his career. He posted career averages of 6 points and 7.9 rebounds per game.

6. MICHAEL CAGE

Michael Cage lasted fifteen NBA seasons based on his rebounding and winning attitude. He led the NBA in rebounding during the 1987–88 season. Heading into the final game of that season, Cage needed 29 rebounds to pass Charles Oakley for the all-time rebounding title. Cage eventually grabbed 30 rebounds to edge Oakley. His career averages were 7.3 points and 7.6 rebounds per game.

7. GEORGE JOHNSON

George Johnson played in thirteen NBA seasons from 1972–1986 because of his defensive skills. A three-time league leader in shot blocking, Johnson posted career averages of 4.8 points and 6.5 rebounds per contest. Johnson was a very limited offensive player whose career field goal average was a paltry 45.1%.

8. ERVIN JOHNSON

At the end of the 2003–04 season, 6′ 11″ center Ervin Johnson had lasted eleven NBA seasons. He posted career averages of 4.3 points and 6.4 rebounds per contest. In his 1996–97 season with the Denver Nuggets (his only season with the Nuggets), Johnson led the league in total number of defensive rebounds. His highest season scoring total was 8 points per game.

9. WILL PERDUE

Will Perdue played thirteen NBA seasons because of his excellent attitude and ability to know and accept his role. For his career, Perdue averaged 4.7 points and 4.9 rebounds per game. Perdue was often a substitute, but he managed to collect four championship rings in his career—three with the Michael Jordan-led Chicago Bulls and one with the San Antonio Spurs.

10. TREE ROLLINS

Wayne "Tree" Rollins played eighteen seasons in the NBA from 1977–1995. A tough defensive presence, Rollins was not ultimately a scorer. He posted career averages of 5.4 points and 5.8 rebounds per game, and he led the league in blocked shots with the Atlanta Hawks in the 1982–83 season.

Small Packages II

*B*asketball's *Most Wanted*™ provided readers with a top-ten list of short players who, nevertheless, made a large impact on the game. But, there are many more players of diminutive size who deserve mention for their athletic ability. All of these players stood under 6′ but stood tall against their competition.

1. SHAWNTA ROGERS

Shawnta Rogers stands only 5′ 4″ inches tall, but that didn't stop him from having a large impact in college basketball for George Washington University. From 1995–1999, Rogers scored more than 1,700 points. In his senior season of 1998–99, Rogers averaged more than 20 points per game and led the nation in steals. His efforts earned him Atlantic 10 Conference Player of the Year honors. In 1999–2000, he played for the Baltimore Bay Runners of the International Basketball League (IBL). In 2003–04, Rogers played professional basketball for Adecco Asvel in France, earning All-Star honors.

2. EARL BOYKINS

Earl Boykins currently plays point guard for the Denver Nuggets. Undrafted out of Eastern Michigan, where he won the Francis Pomeroy Naismith award, the 5′ 5″ Boykins has also played for the New Jersey Nets, Cleveland Cavaliers, Orlando Magic, Los Angeles Clippers, and the Golden State Warriors. He continues to confound opposing teams with his amazing quickness and clutch shooting. He came into his own with the Warriors in 2002–03, averaging nearly 9 points a game and getting in huge chunks of playing time during the fourth quarter when games were on the line. In 2003–04, Boykins played in all 82 games for the Nuggets and averaged more than 10 points a game.

3. KEITH JENNINGS

Keith "Mister" Jennings starred at East Tennessee State University, leading the team to several NCAA tournament bids. From 1987–1991, the 5′ 7″ Jennings scored 1,989 points. His senior year, he averaged more than 20 points per game, led the nation in three-point accuracy, and earned Second Team All-America honors. For his efforts, he was named the Frances Pomeroy Naismith award winner—given to the outstanding college senior 6′ or under. Jennings played two seasons for the Golden State Warriors in 1993–94 and 1994–95 seasons. As of 2004, he still plays professional basketball overseas.

4. MONTE TOWE

The 5′ 7″ Towe started 86 consecutive games as point guard for the North Carolina Wolfpack. He led the Wolfpack with David Thompson and Tom Burleson to the

NCAA title in 1974, and in 1975 he captured the Frances Pomeroy Naismith award. Upon graduation, Towe played two seasons for the Denver Nuggets. After his playing days ended, Towe turned to coaching and is now the head basketball coach of the University of New Orleans Privateers.

5. CHARLIE CRISS

Charlie Criss played for parts of eight NBA seasons from 1977 until 1983 for the Atlanta Hawks, San Diego Clippers and Milwaukee Bucks. The 5' 8" Criss was undrafted after his college career at New Mexico State. However, Criss persevered and became an NBA rookie at the age of 28. In his first season with the Hawks, Criss averaged more than 11 points per game. In 2004, Criss served as the director of the Atlanta Hawks Summer Basketball Camp.

6. LARRY BROWN

When people think of Larry Brown, they think of the highly successful coach who led Kansas to the NCAA championship and the Detroit Pistons to the 2003–04 NBA title. But Larry Brown was a great point guard in college for the University of North Carolina, and then for the New Orleans Buccaneers, Oakland Oaks, and Washington Capitals of the ABA. The 5' 9" Brown led the ABA in assists for the first three years of the league's existence. He made the second All-Star team in 1967–68, and was the most valuable player in the 1968 ABA All-Star game, coming off the bench to score 17 points and dish out 5 assists.

7. JOHN WOODEN

John Wooden is known as the greatest coach in the history of college basketball. His UCLA Bruins became a dynasty in college basketball, winning seven straight NCAA titles. Before his legendary coaching, Wooden was also a great basketball player. At Purdue University, the 5′ 10″ Wooden became the first player to be named a consensus All-American three years in a row from 1930–1932.

8.   TYUS EDNEY

Tyus Edney will be best remembered for his coast-to-coast, last-second shot over the University of Missouri in the second round of the 1995 NCAA tournament to help his UCLA Bruins escape with a win. With only 4.8 seconds left in the game and the Bruins down by 1 point, the 5′ 10″ Edney raced the length of the court to score and capture the win. UCLA then went on to win the national championship. That year, Edney earned the Frances Pomeroy Naismith award for his stellar season. Edney played four seasons in the NBA with the Sacramento Kings, the Boston Celtics, and the Indiana Pacers. He now plays professional basketball in Europe.

9.   BREVIN KNIGHT

Brevin Knight starred at Stanford University from 1993 until 1997, amassing more than 1,700 points. His senior year he earned All-America honors and captured the Frances Pomeroy Naismith award. A first-round draft pick for the Cleveland Cavaliers, Knight has played eight years in the NBA. In 2004–05, Knight played for the Charlotte Bobcats and finished second in the league in assists. He is known for his tenacious, on-the-ball defense and ability to penetrate.

10.   MICHAEL ADAMS

Michael Adams scored 1,650 points for the Boston College Eagles from 1981–1985. He played eleven seasons in the NBA with the Sacramento Kings, the Washington Bullets, the Denver Nuggets, and the Charlotte Hornets. Adams was a nightmare to defend because of his blazing quickness and shot-put three pointers. In the 1990–91 season with the Nuggets, Adams averaged 26.5 points per game and dished out 10.5 assists. Adams holds an NBA record for making at least one three-point shot in 79 consecutive games, and he once scored 54 points in a single game. He coached the Washington Mystics of the WNBA. He currently is an assistant coach with Maryland.

Same Name Game

Many trivia experts like to play the name game and here is a list to whet their appetites. The following names were shared by multiple pro basketball players.

1. CHARLES SMITH

Three men named Charles Smith played in the NBA. The best known was Charles Daniel Smith, the 6′ 10″ forward out of the University of Pittsburgh who played for the Los Angeles Clippers, New York Knicks, and San Antonio Spurs between 1988 and 1997. He averaged more than 20 points per game in two different seasons in his pro career. Charles Cornelius Smith played parts of five seasons from 1997–2003 with several teams. The 6′ 4″ guard out of New Mexico started only 32 games in his career. Finally, Charles Edward Smith IV played parts of three seasons (89–90, 90–91, and 95–96) in the NBA with the Boston Celtics and the Minnesota Timberwolves. The 6′ 1″ guard out of Georgetown played in a total of 73 NBA games.

2. CHARLES JONES

Three men named Charles Jones also played in the NBA. The longest career belonged to the 6′ 9″ forward out of Albany State. This Jones played from 1983 until 1997 with five different teams. A defensive stopper, he averaged only 1.5 points and 2.5 rebounds per game. Charles Rahmel Jones was a 6′ 3″ guard out of Long Island University. At Long Island, the sharp-shooting Jones led the NCAA in scoring for the 1996–97 and 1997–98 seasons, averaging nearly 30 points per game. Unfortunately, Jones never could match his collegiate scoring in the NBA, as he averaged only 3.5 points per game in two seasons with the Chicago Bulls and Los Angeles Clippers. Charles Alexander Jones was a high-leaping 6′ 8″ forward out of the University of Louisville who played professionally from 1984–1988. He averaged 5 points and nearly 4 rebounds a game.

3.   GEORGE JOHNSON

There were three George Johnsons who played in the NBA as well. The first was George E. Johnson, a 6′ 11″ center out of Stephen F. Austin State. He played four years with three different teams from 1970–1974, averaging less than 3 points per game. The next was George Thomas Johnson, who played from 1972 until 1986. He led the league in blocked shots in three seasons, and played for seven teams in his long career. Finally, George L. Johnson played parts of eight seasons with five different teams from 1978–1985. A 6′ 7″ forward out of St. John's University, he averaged more than 9 points per game.

4.   EDDIE JOHNSON

Edward Johnson, Jr. was better known by the nickname "Fast Eddie," for his amazing quickness on the basketball court. The point guard from Auburn University played nearly nine of his ten NBA seasons with the

Atlanta Hawks. He averaged as many as 19 points per game in his prime.

Edward Arnet Johnson, known simply as Eddie Johnson, enjoyed a longer NBA career that stretched from 1981–1998. The sweet-shooting small forward was known for his deadly outside shot. Three times in his career—twice with the Kansas City Kings and once with the Phoenix Suns—he averaged more than 20 points per game in a season. During the 1988–89 season Johnson won the Sixth Man of the Year award, averaging 21.5 points per game for the Suns off the bench.

5. BILL BRADLEY

Most basketball fans and the American public recognize the name of former Princeton and New York Knick basketball great Bill Bradley. He was an All-American, a Hall of Famer, a U.S. Senator, and later a presidential candidate in 2000. But, there was another Bill Bradley who played professional basketball. This Bradley starred at Tennessee State before playing with the Kentucky Colonels during the 1968–69 season. He averaged more than 9 points per game in his only season.

6. JOHN WILLIAMS

John Williams was the name of two solid NBA players who entered the pro ranks in the same year—1986. John "Hot Rod" Williams was a 6′ 11″ forward-center out of Tulane who played thirteen seasons in the league. He was a star Sixth Man for the Cleveland Cavaliers, and he averaged double figures in scoring all seven years. John Sam Williams was a bulky 6′ 8″ forward out of Louisiana State University who never quite reached his potential with the Washington Bullets, Los

Angeles Clippers, or Indiana Pacers. He still managed to average more than 10 points per game in his eight-year pro career.

7. **ROGER BROWN**

Though he began his pro career at the ripe age of 25, Roger A. Brown was one of the greatest players in the history of the ABA. For the first five years of his pro career with the Indiana Pacers, Brown was perhaps the league's best small forward. He averaged 17.4 points per game for his eight-year career. In the 1970 championship series, Brown averaged 32.7 points and 10 rebounds per game, including a 53-point outburst. There was another Roger Brown who played professional basketball in the NBA and ABA from 1972–1980. He stood 6' 11" and played collegiately at Kansas. Brown was a bench player whose best season scoring average was 5 points per game.

8. **LARRY JOHNSON**

Most NBA fans will remember the Larry Johnson who was a 6' 6" undersized power forward out of UNLV who starred for the Charlotte Hornets and New York Knicks from 1991–2001. In his beginning years he teamed with Alonzo Mourning to give the Hornets a dangerous inside duo. Johnson averaged more than 20 points per game in two separate seasons. After knee surgery, Johnson was never quite the same player, though he later expanded his range to the three-point line with the New York Knicks. There was another Larry Johnson who played in the NBA. This Larry Johnson was a 6' 3" guard out of Kentucky who played in four NBA games with the Buffalo Braves in the 1977–78 season. He averaged 9.5 points in just those few games.

9. CHARLES DAVIS

Charles Lawrence, or Charlie, Davis played in the NBA from 1971 through 1974 with the Cleveland Cavaliers and the Portland Trailblazers. A 6′ 2″ guard from Wake Forest, he averaged 9 points per game in his career. Charles Edward Davis, Jr. played eight seasons in the NBA from 1981–1990. The 6′ 7″ forward out of Vanderbilt played for the Washington Bullets, the Milwaukee Bucks, the San Antonio Spurs, and the Chicago Bulls. He averaged more than 5 points per game in his career.

10. CLIFF ROBINSON

Two players named Cliff Robinson have played in the NBA. Clifford Trent Robinson played from 1979–1992 after a college career at USC. He posted a career scoring average of 17.2 points per game and a season high of 20.2 with the Kansas City Kings. Clifford Ralph Robinson has played fifteen seasons and counting for several teams, including the Portland Trailblazers, the Phoenix Suns, the Detroit Pistons, and the Golden State Warriors. He averaged more than 20 points per game for three seasons in a row with Portland.

Their Rookie Years Were Their Best

Most players getting started at the professional level have some growing pains on and off the court. As one might expect, it takes time for players to adapt to the grueling, 82-game professional schedule. However, these ten players were different because their finest seasons were their rookie seasons. For one reason or another, they were never able to match the numbers they put up in their initial seasons.

1. SPENCER HAYWOOD

Spencer Haywood was pro basketball's original hardship case, leaving the University of Detroit after his sophomore year for the professional ranks. Haywood's best year was his first with the Denver Nuggets in the ABA. Haywood led the league with 30.8 points and 19.5 rebounds per game. His performance earned him both Rookie of the Year and Most Valuable Player honors. He moved to the NBA the next year, and though he had some great seasons, he never equaled the lofty totals of his rookie year.

2.   **WALT BELLAMY**

Walt "Bells" Bellamy had an incredible rookie season with the Chicago Bulls in 1961–62. He averaged 31.6 points and 19 rebounds per game, and managed a league-leading 51.1 shooting percentage from the field. His performance that year earned him Rookie of the Year honors. Bellamy had a Hall-of-Fame, fourteen-year career but he never scored as many points or grabbed as many rebounds as he did in his first year.

3.   **WALTER DAVIS**

A sweet-shooting Walter "The Greyhound" Davis teamed with Paul Westphal to become the "Guns of the Suns" for three years in the late 1970s. Davis played eleven years for the Suns in his 15-year career. His best year statistically came in his rookie season of 1977–78. That year, Davis averaged an amazing 24.2 points and 6 rebounds per game—both career highs. His performance earned him Rookie of the Year honors.

4.   **BILL CARTWRIGHT**

Bill Cartwright was an awkward 7′ 1″ center who helped lead the Chicago Bulls to three NBA titles in the early 1990s. Cartwright was a role player and defensive stopgap for the Bulls, but in his early years with the New York Knicks, Cartwright was an offensive force. His best year statistically was his rookie season of 1979–80. He averaged a career-high 21.7 points and 8.9 rebounds in more than 38 minutes per game.

5.   **JAY VINCENT**

Jay Vincent was a high-scoring forward for the Dallas Mavericks in the early 1980s, who was overshadowed by teammates Mark Aguirre and Rolando Blackman. Vincent, who played at Michigan State with Earvin "Magic" Johnson, scored 21.4 points per game in his rookie campaign of 1981–82. It was the only time Vincent ever averaged more than 20 points per game in his nine-year career.

6. ALVAN ADAMS

Alvan Adams played thirteen years with the Phoenix Suns from 1975–1988. In his rookie season he averaged 19 points, 9.1 rebounds, and 5.6 assists per game. His performance that year earned him Rookie of the Year honors.

7. FREDDIE BOYD

Freddie Boyd played seven years in the NBA with the Philadelphia 76ers and the New Orleans Jazz. A 6′ 2″ guard out of Oregon State, Boyd's most productive year was his first. In his rookie year, Boyd had career highs in minutes played, points per game, rebounds per game, and assists per game. His first year was the only year of his pro career that he averaged double figures in scoring. He posted a career scoring average of 8.5 points per game.

8. TYUS EDNEY

The lightning-quick Tyus Edney played four years in the NBA beginning in 1995. His best year by far as a professional was in his rookie year with the Sacramento Kings. He started 60 games that year, tallying 10.8 points and 6.1 assists per game. He started only 27 more games the rest of his career.

9. MATEEN CLEAVES

Mateen Cleaves's has never reached the greatness expected of his pro career after he guided the Michigan

State Spartans to the NCAA crown in 2000. Cleaves's best year was his rookie season with Detroit, when he played 16 minutes per game, and tallied 5 points and nearly 3 assists per game. In other pro seasons he has failed to average even 5 minutes per game.

10. ELSTON TURNER

Elston Turner was a high-scoring machine out of the University of Mississippi, but he wasn't able to score at nearly the same rate in the NBA. In his rookie year of 1981–82 with the Dallas Mavericks, Turner averaged 25 minutes and 8.3 points per game. The next highest scoring average in his eight-year pro career was 5.1. He started 62 games in his rookie year, while he started only 35 games in his next seven years.

Player-Coaches

Occasionally in professional basketball, a team has chosen or has been forced to have one of its own players coach the team. For instance, the Virginia Squires in the ABA were in such bad financial shape that they had two different players coach their team during the 1975–76 season—Mack Calvin and Willie Wise. The following ten players were player-coaches in the professional ranks.

1. HARRY "BUDDY" JEANETTE

Harry "Buddy" Jeanette was the first player-coach to win a professional basketball championship in 1947. That year he led the Baltimore Bullets to the title in the American Basketball League (ABL). The next year, the Bullets left the ABL to join the Basketball Association of America (BAA). Jeanette again served as player-coach and led the Bullets to the 1948 BAA championship over the Philadelphia Warriors. He remains one of two men—along with Bill Russell—to serve as player-coach and win a pro basketball championship.

2. **LENNY WILKENS**

Lenny Wilkens is the only person inducted in the Basketball Hall of Fame for his success as an NBA player (1989) and an NBA coach (1998). From 1969 to 1972, Wilkens served as both point guard and coach for the Seattle Supersonics. He also served as player-coach for the Portland Trailblazers during the 1974–75 season. Wilkens guided the Seattle Supersonics to the 1979 NBA title as a coach (but not as a player) and holds the record for the most coaching victories in the NBA.

3. **BILL RUSSELL**

Bill Russell was the centerpiece of the great Boston Celtics dynasty, leading the team to 11 NBA titles in thirteen years. For his final two championships, Russell had the honor of serving as player-coach and is recognized as the first player-coach to win an NBA title.

4. **CLIFF HAGAN**

Cliff Hagan was an All-Star and a Hall of Famer who earned recognition for his success at the University of Kentucky. He then went on to earn numerous All-Star honors for his accomplishments with the St. Louis Hawks. From 1967 to 1970, Hagan served as player-coach for the ABA's Dallas Chapparels. In his first game as player-coach, Hagan scored 40 points. He played in the ABA's first All-Star game.

5. **AL CERVI**

Al Cervi was inducted into the Basketball Hall of Fame as a tribute to his great playing days in the National

Basketball League (NBL) and the NBA. The 5′ 11″ guard earned MVP honors in the NBL for his great play with the Syracuse Nationals. From 1948 to 1953, Cervi served as player-coach for the Nationals, earning coach of the year honors in 1949. He compiled a record of 210–120 as a player-coach.

6. RICHIE GUERIN

Richie Guerin was an outstanding player in the NBA, averaging as many as 29.5 points per game in the 1961–62 season and playing in five All-Star games. Guerin served as player-coach for the St. Louis Hawks for three seasons, from 1964 to 1967. The franchise moved to Atlanta in 1967, where he served as player-coach for two more years. He coached until 1972, compiling a 327–291 record.

7. DAVE DeBUSSCHERE

Dave DeBusschere played a key role on the New York Knicks championship teams in 1970 and 1973. De-Busschere later served as commissioner of the ABA for two seasons. He became the youngest player-coach in basketball history, at 24 years old, when he was hired to coach the Detroit Pistons in 1964. He served in the role of player-coach for three seasons, compiling a losing record of 79–143.

8. KEVIN LOUGHERY

Kevin Loughery was a hard-nosed player who twice averaged more than 20 points per game with the Baltimore Bullets. Loughery ended his playing days during the 1972–73 season as a player-coach with the Philadelphia 76ers. The team did not fare well and Loughery posted an abysmal mark of 5–26. Loughery rebounded to coach Julius Erving and the New York Nets to two ABA championships. He was also Michael Jordan's first professional coach with the Chicago Bulls.

9. DAVE COWENS

Dave Cowens was a hustling, whirling dervish of a center. Though undersized for the position at 6' 9", Cowens played with remarkable energy and earned seven All-Star appearances. During the 1978–79 season with the Celtics, Cowens assumed the role of player-coach, replacing Satch Sanders after 14 games. The Celtics went 27–41 with Cowens as player-coach, and he later coached the Charlotte Hornets and the Golden State Warriors.

10. WILLIAM ROBERT "SLICK" LEONARD

Slick Leonard played seven seasons in the NBA, ending his career as player-coach for the Chicago Zephyrs in the 1962–63 season. Leonard's record as player-coach was 13–29, but he rebounded nicely as a coach when he guided the Indiana Pacers to three ABA championships in the 1970s. He earned more victories in the history of the ABA than any other coach.

Their College Teams Lost But They Won Top Honors

The NCAA Final Four is arguably the biggest stage in basketball, even greater than the NBA Finals. Normally, a player from the winning team captures the Most Outstanding Player award. In fact, the last player to win the MOP award from a losing team was more than twenty years ago. These ten players won top individual honors even though their teams lost.

1. WILT CHAMBERLAIN

In the 1957 NCAA championship, the North Carolina Tarheels defeated sophomore Wilt Chamberlain and the Kansas Jayhawks in triple overtime, 54–53. Tarheel coach Frank McGuire used slowdown tactics and surrounded Chamberlain with several players to try to stop the goliath scoring machine. Chamberlain still managed 23 points and 14 rebounds in defeat. For his two games in the Final Four, Chamberlain collected 55 points and 25 rebounds. He was named MOP.

2. ELGIN BAYLOR

In the 1958 NCAA championship, the University of Kentucky defeated Seattle University 84–72 to win the title. Kentucky focused most of their attention on Seattle's junior forward Elgin Baylor and limited him to 9 for 32 shooting. Baylor still managed 25 points and 19 rebounds in the contest. For his two games in the Final Four, he tallied 48 points and grabbed 41 rebounds. Despite his poor shooting performance in the championship game, he was named MOP of the Final Four.

3. BILL BRADLEY

Princeton's Bill Bradley won the MOP award of the 1965 Final Four, even though his team did not reach the championship game. In the consolation game against Wichita State, Bradley poured in an NCAA Final Four–record 58 points. For his two games in the Final Four, Bradley scored an incredible 87 points and grabbed 24 rebounds. It was only the third time in NCAA history that the MOP award went to a player that did not participate in the championship game. It won't be duplicated any time soon, either, as the NCAA no longer offers a consolation game.

4. JERRY WEST

In the 1959 NCAA championships, the University of California defeated West Virginia 71–70. The defeat was a bitter one for West Virginia's Jerry West, who put up 28 points and 11 rebounds. For the two games, West scored 65 points and grabbed 25 rebounds and was named the Final Four's MOP.

5. HAKEEM OLAJUWON

Hakeem Olajuwon's heavily-favored Houston Cougars lost 54–52 to coach Jim Valvano's North Carolina State Wolfpack on a last-second dunk by Lorenzo Charles. Olajuwon dominated the paint for much of the game with 20 points and 18 rebounds. For his efforts, he was named the Final Four's MOP. Olajuwon was the last player from a losing team to win the award.

6. JIMMY HULL

In the inaugural NCAA championship in 1939, Oregon defeated Ohio State 46–33. Despite the defeat, Ohio State's Jimmy Hull captured MOP honors. In his two Final Four games, the senior Hull scored 40 points: 28 points in the semifinal game and 12 in the final against Oregon.

7. HAL LEAR

In the 1956 NCAA championship, San Francisco defeated Iowa 83–71 to win the title. However, the MOP in the Final Four was not from either San Francisco or Iowa. Rather, it was Temple's Hal Lear. Lear scored 32 points in the semifinal game against Iowa and then a whopping 48 points against Southern Methodist in the consolation game. Lear's two-game total of 80 points ranks second to Bradley's 87. Lear became the first player to win MOP honors even though he did not participate in the championship game.

8. JERRY LUCAS

In the 1961 NCAA championship game, Cincinnati defeated Ohio State 70–65 in overtime to spoil the Buckeyes' chances of a repeat title. Even though his team lost, Jerry Lucas captured MOP honors, just as he did the year before when Ohio State won the title. Lucas scored 27 points and grabbed 11 rebounds in the '61 championship game.

9. ART HEYMAN

In the 1963 NCAA championship, Loyola of Chicago upset Cincinnati 60–58 in overtime to win the title. The

MOP of the Final Four was not from either championship team, however. Art Heyman of Duke University was selected for his two-game total of 51 points and 19 rebounds. He became the second player to win the MOP award despite not having played in the championship game.

10.   **JERRY CHAMBERS**

In the controversial (at the time) 1966 NCAA championship, Texas-El Paso made history by defeating the University of Kentucky 72–65. Texas-El Paso went down in the record books by starting five African American players against Adolph Rupp's all-white Kentucky team. But Jerry Chambers of Utah captured the MOP award, even though his Utah squad lost both a semifinal game to Loyola and the consolation game to Duke. Chambers scored 70 points and grabbed 35 rebounds in the two games. He is the only player in NCAA history to win top individual honors in the Final Four while playing for the fourth place team.

Married to Stars

Professional basketball players are celebrities in this modern star-worshipping culture. Many NBA stars meet celebrities from other walks of life in the entertainment industry, so it shouldn't come as a surprise that several NBA players have dated and married celebrities.

1. RICK FOX

This former Los Angeles Lakers forward is married to the talented and beautiful Vanessa L. Williams. Williams won the coveted Miss America title in 1983, but she was stripped of her title for nude photographs of herself published in Penthouse Magazine. The controversy did not affect Williams's career, and she has achieved great success as both a singer and an actress.

2. GRANT HILL

Grant Hill is the multi-talented forward who played with the Detroit Pistons and now plays with the Orlando Magic. In 1999, he married the talented singer Tamia Lee Washington, known by her first name Tamia. Tamia has earned three Grammy nominations for songs such as "Slow Jams" with Babyface and "Missing You" with Gladys Knight, Chaka Khan, and Brandy.

3. DENNIS RODMAN

Dennis Rodman was a unique, energetic forward who played a key role on two championship teams with the Detroit Pistons and then three more championships with the Chicago Bulls. He made waves in gossip columns and elsewhere for dating pop icon Madonna, and in November 1998, Rodman married model-actress Carmen Electra. The marriage did not end in happy bliss, as Electra filed for divorce in April 1999.

4. NORM NIXON

Norm Nixon was a star guard in the 1970s and 1980s with the Los Angeles Lakers, and then with the Los Angeles Clippers. Nixon married famed celebrity Debbie Allen in 1984, and the couple has two children. Allen achieved prominence for her creation of the 1982 hit movie *Fame*, which she both directed and starred in. She has also been the director of such television hits as *The Parkers* and *The Jamie Foxx Show*. Allen is the sister of *Cosby Show* star and Tony award-winner Phylicia Rashad.

5. MARK JACKSON

Mark Jackson is one of the great passing point guards in NBA history. He earned fame and his only All-Star appearance early in his career with the New York Knicks. Jackson married actress-singer Desiree Coleman. Coleman, known as Dez, is an accomplished Broadway performer and singer. She has opened for

R&B legend Patti LaBelle, and in 2001 she released a Christian music album entitled *Sing For Me.*

6. RICKY PIERCE

Ricky Pierce, the former Sixth Man specialist (shooting guard, sometimes small forward) for the Milwaukee Bucks, twice won the NBA's Sixth Man of the Year award. He made the NBA All-Star team even though he never started for his own team. Pierce's wife Joyce is also a star. She is a former singer with the popular music group Fifth Dimension. In February 1987, Joyce sang the national anthem at one of her husband's games. Apparently inspired, Pierce went out and hit 11 of 14 shots and tallied a then-career high 32 points. His coach, Don Nelson, said to the Associated Press of Pierce's wife: "She can sing anytime she wants to."

7. RONY SEIKALY

Rony Seikaly starred at Syracuse University and then played nearly a dozen years in the NBA. In five of his first six seasons, he averaged double figures in both points and rebounds. A native of Beirut, Lebanon, Seikaly married top model Elsa Benitez in 1999. Benitez graced the cover of *Sports Illustrated's* popular Swimsuit Issue in 2001. Seikaly has said of going out with his stunningly beautiful wife in public: "I'm more of a bodyguard than a husband."

8. JOHN BATTLE

John Battle played ten years in the NBA as a shooting guard for the Atlanta Hawks and the Cleveland Cavaliers. Battle was often instant offense off the bench, averaging double figures in four seasons. In 1991, Battle married recording star Regina Belle. Belle, a Grammy nominee, has recorded such hits as "Baby Come to Me," "Make It Like It Was," and "A Whole New World" (the theme song of the Disney movie *Aladdin*).

9. GREG ANTHONY

Greg Anthony played twelve seasons in the NBA for six different teams from 1991 to 2002. A former star at UNLV, Anthony was best known for his aggressive play and tenacious defense. He now has a successful career as an NBA analyst for ESPN. His wife, Carla McCrary-Anthony, is a successful writer. She has co-authored two hit books: *Homecourt Advantage* with Rita Ewing, the former wife of basketball player Patrick Ewing, and *Gotham Diaries: A Novel* with Tonya Lewis Lee, the wife of movie producer Spike Lee.

10. JASON KIDD

Jason Kidd is the point guard for the New Jersey Nets. A perennial All-Star, Kidd is regularly among the league leaders in assists, steals and triple doubles. His wife, Joumana Kidd, has a burgeoning career in television news. In 2002 she began working as a national correspondent for the entertainment TV program *Extra*, and is also a television reporter for NBA Entertainment. In 2001 she starred in the movie *Whiplash*, which was shown at the Sundance Film Festival.

Legal Stars

Some basketball players have possessed both brains and brawn. Many have exchanged the basketball court for another arena—the court of law. For example, the NBA's first great center, George Mikan, obtained a law degree from his undergraduate alma mater, DePaul University. The following is a list of ten such individuals who starred both in basketball and in law.

1. **MORRIS K. UDALL**

Morris Udall's middle name was King, and he lived a life of regal accomplishments. A young Udall lost his right eye at age seven, but he still became a great basketball player at the University of Arizona. His college career was interrupted from 1942 through 1945 for service in World War II, but he returned to the university to captain the basketball team and earn not only his bachelor's degree but also a law degree. The 6′ 5″ Udall then played one year of professional basketball for the Denver Nuggets of the NBA, averaging 6.5 points per game. In 1961 he was elected to the U.S. House of

Representatives and served an amazing sixteen terms. He ran for the Democratic presidential nomination in 1976, finishing second to future president Jimmy Carter.

2. JOHN ROCHE

John Roche was a two-time ACC Player of the Year for the University of South Carolina, where he played point guard for three seasons from 1969 to 1971. Roche then played professional basketball for eight seasons, first in the ABA and then in the NBA with the Denver Nuggets. Remarkably, Roche attended law school and graduated while playing ball professionally. In 1981, Roche became the first licensed attorney to play in the NBA. Roche is now an attorney with the law firm of Snell & Wilmer L.L.P. in Denver.

3. R. MALCOLM GRAHAM

R. Malcolm, or "Mal", Graham played college basketball at New York University and was drafted in the first round by the Boston Celtics. Graham, a 6' 1" guard, played two years for the Celtics during the 1967–68 and 1968–69 seasons. Graham next sought a legal career, earning his law degree from Boston College in 1974. He was appointed to a Massachusetts district judgeship in 1982, and to the Superior Court in 1986. He has served as president of the Massachusetts Black Judges Association and received a Judicial Excellence Award from the Massachusetts Judges Conference in 1998.

4. SONJA HENNING

Sonja Henning led the Stanford Cardinals to the women's NCAA title in 1990, before embarking on a professional basketball career that included time in Sweden. Henning then earned a law degree from Duke University. She tried out for the ABL in 1996 while still a practicing attorney, and for many years she played professional basketball and practiced law in the off-season. She starred on the 1999 Houston Comets' championship team, and then played for the Seattle Storm and the Indiana Fever. She retired in 2003 and practices law full-time for the law firm of Tonkin Torp L.L.P.

5.   LEN ELMORE

Len Elmore was an All-American during his career at the University of Maryland, which included three All-Conference seasons. He then played ten years of professional basketball—two in the ABA and eight in the NBA. After retiring in 1984, Elmore attended the University of Harvard Law School. He earned his law degree in 1987 and became an assistant district attorney in Brooklyn, New York. Elmore then founded a sports agency company, and later, an online test preparation company. He now serves as a college basketball announcer for ESPN.

6.   VALERIE ACKERMAN

Valerie Ackerman was a star basketball player for the University of Virginia from 1977 to 1981. She was captain of the squad for three years and a four-year starter. In addition, she was a two-time Academic All-American. After graduation, Ackerman played a year of professional basketball in France. She then went to law school at UCLA where she graduated in 1985. After two years with a New York law firm, Ackerman became a staff attorney for the NBA in 1988, and later she became special assistant to NBA commissioner David

Stern. In 1996, she was selected as the president of the WNBA.

7. **JAMES BURNS**

Jim Burns was a star at Northwestern University from 1964 to 1967. When he graduated, he was the school's all-time leading scorer. Burns went on to play one season of professional basketball with the Dallas Chapparels in the ABA, and then played briefly for the Chicago Bulls during the 1967–68 season. Burns returned to Northwestern to earn his law degree, and from 1993 to 1997 Burns served as U.S. attorney for the Northern District of Illinois. In 2000, he became Illinois's Inspector General.

8. **ANN KIRWIN ANDERSON**

Ann Kirwin Anderson was a star basketball player for Bucknell University, graduating in 1987. After Graduation she played professionally for two years in Germany. When she ended her basketball career, Anderson went to law school and earned a degree from the University of Connecticut in 1994. She was a law professor at Quinnepac Law School, and at her alma mater Connecticut. In 1998 she was inducted into Bucknell's Sports Hall of Fame.

9. **BARRY GOHEEN**

Barry Goheen scored more than 1,500 points in a four-year career with the Vanderbilt Commodores, from 1985 to 1989. But it was his timing and flare that enshrined him in SEC basketball history. Goheen had an uncanny knack for hitting buzzer-beater shots, some from amazing distances. In November 1988, Goheen hit a 45-footer at the buzzer to lift the Commodores over the nationally ranked Louisville Cardinals. After his college career, Goheen worked for two years before attending law school at Vanderbilt University Law School. He worked at the Nashville law firm of Boult Cummings, then transferred to the nationally known Atlanta firm of King & Spalding.

10. PERRY WALLACE JR.

Perry Wallace Jr. made history by becoming the first African American basketball player in the history of the SEC when he joined the Vanderbilt Commodores in 1966. He was an All-Star player for the Commodores, scoring more than 1,000 points in his three-year career. Wallace later earned a law degree from Columbia University in 1975. He is now a law professor at American University's Washington College of Law. He teaches courses in Environmental Law, Business Associations, Law and Accounting, and Securities Regulation.

They Turned Their Teams Around

Sometimes a single individual—whether a player or a coach—can seemingly turn around an entire team's fortune. They become the spark that lights the fire of success. Whether through individual talent, motivational skills, or other intangible qualities, the following ten individuals turned their teams around in a positive direction.

1. BILL LAIMBEER

In 2002, the Detroit Shock stumbled to an anemic record of 9–23—the worst record in the WNBA. However, in their first full season under coach Bill Laimbeer a former stalwart on the Detroit Pistons' championship teams the Shock electrified the basketball world by finishing with a league-best record of 25–9. The Shock topped off their magical year by beating the defending champion Los Angeles Sparks to win the title. It was a true worst-to-first finish. Star center Ruth Riley, the MVP of the championship series, perhaps said it best: "It all starts with Coach."

2. PHIL JACKSON

For several years, the Los Angeles Lakers possessed perhaps the best talent in the NBA, but they could not seem to live up to their potential. In the 1998–99 season they were swept 4–0 by the San Antonio Spurs in the Western Conference semifinals. In the off-season, the Lakers hired former Chicago Bull coach, Phil Jackson. Jackson, or "Zen Master" as he is called, made an immediate impact on Shaquille O'Neal, Kobe Bryant, and the rest of the Lakers. Under Jackson's leadership the Lakers posted an NBA-best record of 67–15, and captured the NBA title with a victory over the Indiana Pacers.

3. LARRY BIRD

Larry Joe Bird made an immediate impact on the Boston Celtics. Prior to Bird's arrival, the Celtics had finished with a dismal record of 29–53. In his rookie season, Bird carried the Celtics to a 61–21 record. He averaged 21.3 points, 10.4 rebounds, and 4.5 assists per game. For his efforts, he won Rookie of the Year honors.

4. TIM DUNCAN

Tim Duncan won the NBA Rookie of the Year award for the 1997–98 season. He helped lead the San Antonio Spurs to a 56–26 record—a 36-game improvement over the previous season when the Spurs suffered a 20–62 record. The Spurs' turnaround is the largest in NBA history from one season to the next. In fairness, part of the team's improvement dealt with David Robinson's return. He had missed 76 games with a back injury.

5. DAVID ROBINSON

In the 1988–89 season, the San Antonio Spurs limped to a 21–61 record. The next year saw David Robinson playing for the Spurs, and he led them to a 56–26 record on his way to capturing Rookie of the Year honors. At the time, the Spurs' 35-game improvement was the largest in NBA history.

6. CARMELO ANTHONY

Carmelo Anthony left Syracuse after leading the Orangemen to an NCAA championship in his freshman season. He made a similar impact on his professional team, the Denver Nuggets. The year before Anthony's arrival, the Nuggets struggled to an anemic 17–65 record. In the 2003–04 season, Anthony helped lead the Nuggets to a 43–39 record—a 26-game improvement over the previous season.

7. HUBIE BROWN

In the 2002–03 season, the Memphis Grizzlies struggled to a 28–54 mark. Then, general manager Jerry West made arguably the best move in franchise history when he hired Hubie Brown as head coach. Brown's ability to teach paid big dividends for the Grizzlies in the 2003–04 season as they won 50 games and made the playoffs for the first time. For his efforts, Brown was named NBA Coach of the Year.

8. LEW ALCINDOR

In the 1968–69 season, the Milwaukee Bucks finished in the cellar of the Eastern Division with a 27–55 record. The next year their number-one draft pick, Lew Alcindor (later Kareem Abdul-Jabbar), took the floor and made an immediate impact. Aided by Alcindor's dominant talents, the Bucks finished the 1969–70 season with a record of 56–26—a 29-game improvement over the previous season.

9. WILT CHAMBERLAIN

In the 1958–59 season, the Philadelphia Warriors finished last in the Eastern Division with a record of 32–40. The next year, Goliath took the court in the form of Wilton Norman Chamberlain. Chamberlain scored 43 points in his debut, and led the Warriors to a 49–26 record. They finished second in the Eastern Division, behind only the mighty Boston Celtics.

10. COTTON FITZSIMMONS

In the 1987–88 season, the Phoenix Suns limped to a 28–54 record. The Suns then hired veteran coach Cotton Fitzsimmons who had coached the team back in the early 1970s. Fitzsimmons earned Coach of the Year honors for guiding the Suns to a 55–27 record—an improvement of 27 games. Fitzsimmons was greatly helped by the free-agent acquisition of forward Tom Chambers from Seattle, who was named to the second team All-NBA.

They Coached
Their Sons

When kids play little league basketball, the coach is often the parent of one of the players. This happens with less and less frequency as players climb the levels of basketball play. However, the following ten coaches had their sons as one of their college basketball players.

1. PRESS and PETE MARAVICH

Press Maravich coached the Louisiana State University Tigers in the late 1960s and early 1970s. In his first season as head coach of LSU, his team finished with a dismal record of 3–23. The next year his son—"Pistol" Pete Maravich—became eligible to play ball in his sophomore season (freshmen were not eligible for the varsity teams then). The team went 14–12, 13–13, and 21–10 in Pistol Pete's three years. Pete set scoring records in his college career that stand to this day. He averaged 43.8, 44.2, and 44.5 points per game in his three seasons with LSU. He is still the all-time scoring leader in NCAA Division I basketball. Maravich went on to become an All-Star player in the professional ranks.

"We win with Pete," Press said. "If he gets special treatment, it's because he is so special."

2. HOMER and BRYCE DREW

Homer Drew coaches the Valparaiso Golden Eagles, and from 1995 to 1998 he had the privilege of coaching his son, Bryce. Bryce Homer Drew was First-Team All-Conference in 1996, 1997, and 1998. In 1998, he scored a dramatic game-winning shot to edge Ole Miss 70–69 and lift Valparaiso to the Sweet Sixteen. Homer still coaches at Valparaiso, coming back after a one-year retirement in 2002. He has been Mid-Continent Conference Coach of the Year four times. Bryce continues to ply his craft in the NBA, playing for the Houston Rockets and then the New Orleans Hornets.

3. TUBBY and SAUL SMITH

Tubby Smith has been a coaching success at several schools, including Tulsa, Georgia, and the University of Kentucky. In his first season at the helm for Kentucky, he won the 1998 NCAA championship. His 2002–03 team finished the SEC season with an unbeaten mark and earned Smith national Coach of the Year honors. His son, Saul Smith, played point guard for the Wildcats from 1997 until 2001. Saul later served as the team's manager after his playing days were over. Tubby also coached his older son, G. G. Smith, at the University of Georgia for two years in 1996 and 1997.

4. BOBBY and PAT KNIGHT

The legendary Bobby Knight coached the Indiana Hoosiers to three NCAA championships and one NIT title during his successful, but oftentimes stormy, tenure as the Hoosiers head. He coached many great players that later starred in the NBA, including Kent Benson, Quinn Buckner, Calbert Cheaney, and Isiah Thomas. But of all the players he coached, it was not hard for him to name his favorite player. "Patrick Knight is my all-time favorite Indiana player," Bobby said. Pat played at Indiana from 1991 to 1995, though he did not see much court time. Pat eventually followed his father into the coaching profession. He has served as an assistant at both Indiana and Texas Tech under his father.

5. JOHN and RONNY THOMPSON

John Thompson coached the Georgetown Hoyas for 27 years, winning 596 games and capturing a national championship in 1984. From 1988 to 1992, his son Ronny was a seldom-used reserve on his Hoyas teams. Ronny was an assistant coach at the University of Oregon, Loyola College in Maryland, and director of scouting for the Philadelphia 76ers. Then in 1998, John Thompson hired his son to join him as an assistant on his staff. John retired in 1999. Ronny is now an assistant basketball coach at the University of Arkansas. Ironically, the current head coach of Georgetown is John's other son, John Thompson III.

6. WADE and ALLAN HOUSTON

Wade Houston coached the University of Tennessee basketball program from 1989 to 1994. He took the position after many years as an assistant at the powerful University of Louisville program under Denny Crum. Unfortunately, Houston's teams struggled at Tennessee, failing to make the NCAA tournament. One bright spot, however, was the spectacular play of Wade's son Allan Houston. Allan became the all-time leading scorer at the University of Tennessee. He played three seasons with the Detroit Pistons and nine seasons with the New York Knicks, and remains one of the game's best pure shooters.

7. **JERRY and DANNY TARKANIAN**

Jerry Tarkanian, a.k.a. "Tark the Shark," coached the UNLV Runnin' Rebels from 1973 until 1992. He led his team to the 1990 NCAA championship, culminating in a 30-point blowout of Duke University. He later coached at his alma mater, Fresno State, from 1995 until 2001. From 1981 to 1984, Danny Tarkanian played three seasons as point guard for his father at UNLV. Danny was a clever passer, amassing assist averages of 8.7, 9.2, and 8.5 per game. He was drafted in the eighth round by the San Antonio Spurs in 1984, and was an assistant coach for his father at both UNLV and Fresno State.

8. **DICK and TONY BENNETT**

Dick Bennett coached Wisconsin–Green Bay from 1985 to 1995, and the University of Wisconsin from 1995 to 2000. He took Wisconsin–Green Bay to the NCAA tournament several times, and he also took the Badgers to the Final Four in 2000. Currently, he coaches the Washington State Cougars. His son, Tony Barrett, was a star guard on his Wisconsin–Green Bay teams from 1988 to 1992, scoring more than 2,200 points in his stellar career. Tony eventually played in the NBA for the Charlotte Hornets. After his playing days were over, he followed his father into coaching. He was an assistant coach at Wisconsin and now serves as an assistant under his father at Washington State.

9. **DON and JERRY MEYER**

Don Meyer has amassed more than 700 wins in thirty seasons as a head basketball coach. He spent twenty-four years coaching National Association of Intercollegiate Athletics (NAIA) ball at David Lipscomb University in Nashville, Tennessee. He won 41 games in the 1989–90 season and captured the NAIA national title in 1986. In the early 1980s, Don coached his son Jerry Meyer at David Lipscomb, where Jerry became college basketball's all-time assist leader. Jerry followed in his father's coaching footsteps, and has served as an assistant at Vanderbilt University. Currently, he coaches high school basketball at Nashville's prestigious Montgomery Bell Academy.

10. **ERNIE and JORDAN KENT**

Ernie Kent coaches basketball at his alma mater the University of Oregon where he graduated in 1977. He has been the head coach at Oregon since 1997 and has taken the Ducks to several NCAA tournaments. His teams play fast-paced, up-and-down offensive game that players such as Luke Ridenour of the Supersonics and Luke Jackson of the Cavaliers excelled at. Kent's youngest son, Jordan, currently plays for the Ducks as a 6′ 5″ guard. Ernie and Jordan aren't the only members of the Kent family that support the Ducks. Ernie's daughter and Jordan's sister McKenzie are cheerleaders for the team. Jordan's brother Marcus—also an OU student—often leads the cheers in the student section.

High School Teammates

O n most high school teams, only a player or two—if that—is skilled enough to play at a higher level. However, some schools have featured so much talent that multiple graduates end up playing not only at the college level, but also at the professional level. These individuals were high school teammates who later played professional basketball in the NBA.

1. **TYRONE BOGUES, DAVID WINGATE, REGGIE WILLIAMS, and REGGIE LEWIS**

NBA players Tyrone "Muggsy" Bogues, David Wingate, Reggie Williams, and Reggie Lewis were all high school teammates at Baltimore's Dunbar High in the mid-1980s. In 1982, the four future professionals led Dunbar to a perfect 28–0 record and a state championship. The next year, Wingate graduated but the other three led Dunbar to a perfect 31–0 mark for coach Bob Wade. Wingate played college ball at Georgetown under John Thompson, then played more than fourteen seasons in the NBA for six different teams. The 5′ 3″ Bogues starred collegiately at Wake Forest and then played fourteen years in the NBA. For most of his career he was the starting point guard for the Charlotte Hornets. Reggie Williams played at Georgetown University and then logged ten years in the NBA. Reggie Lewis played at Northeastern and then six seasons for the Boston Celtics. Lewis died tragically in 1993 at the height of his career, having just completed a season in which he averaged more than 20 points per game.

2. **JALEN ROSE, VOSHON LEONARD, and HOWARD EISLEY**

NBA players Jalen Rose, Voshon Leonard, and Howard Eisley were all teammates at Southwestern High School in Detroit, Michigan. The teammates, coached by Perry Watson, won state championships in 1990 and 1991. Their team was undefeated in 1990 and won *USA Today's* mythical national championship for high school basketball teams (there is no actual national tournament for high school teams). Rose starred at the University of Michigan as part of the famed Fab Five recruiting class that won two straight NCAA championships. Rose now stars for the Toronto Raptors. Leonard starred at Minnesota in college, and in 2003–04 he was the starting shooting guard for the Denver Nuggets. Eisley served as John Stockton's backup during the Utah Jazz's two trips to the NBA championship series against Michael Jordan's Chicago Bulls. In the 2003–04 season, he played for the New York Knicks.

3. **KEITH LEE and MICHAEL CAGE**

Keith Lee and Michael Cage were teammates for West Memphis High School in West Memphis, Arkansas. In 1980, Lee and Cage led their team to a 30–0 record and the state championship. In the championship game, West Memphis defeated Little Rock Central 75–74 on a last-second shot by Aaron Price, a reserve. Lee starred at Memphis State, earning All-American honors. He played only three years in the NBA before knee injuries forced his retirement. Cage played college basketball at San Diego State, and then played fifteen seasons in the NBA. He led the league in rebounding in the 1987–88 season.

4.   TYSON CHANDLER and TAYSHAUN PRINCE

Tyson Chandler and Tayshaun Prince were teammates for one year at Dominguez High School in Compton, California. The two played together when Prince was a senior and the 7' Chandler was a freshman. Though they had previously won two straight state championships, the team lost in the regionals to prevent a three-peat in 1997–98. Chandler and Prince both joined the NBA ranks in different ways. Prince went the more traditional route, starring at the University of Kentucky. He then moved up to the Detroit Pistons and played a key role on the championship team in 2003–04. Chandler skipped college and went straight to the NBA. He has played several seasons with the Chicago Bulls.

5.   GARY PAYTON and GREG FOSTER

Gary Payton and Greg Foster were teammates at Skyline High School in Oakland, California, in the mid-1980s. During their junior and senior years, the team went 39–12 against tough competition. Ironically, college scouts were more interested in the taller Foster than in Payton. Foster starred at UCLA before playing many years in the NBA as a reserve; in only one NBA season has Foster ever started more than 10 games. Payton, on the other hand, had a Hall of Fame career with the Seattle Supersonics. In the 2003–04 season he became a member of the Los Angeles Lakers. Called "The Glove," Payton has been considered one of the best point guards of his era.

6. MILT WAGNER and BILLY THOMPSON

Milt Wagner and Billy Thompson were not only high school, but also college and professional teammates. Wagner was one year ahead of Thompson at Camden High School in Camden, New Jersey. In the 1980–81 season, the senior Wagner and junior Thompson led Camden with a high-powered offense that averaged more than 100 points per game. Wagner then went on to the University of Louisville. Thompson followed the next year, creating what sportswriters and others called "The Camden Connection." Wagner and Thompson were both senior members of Louisville's national championship team in 1986 (Wagner had redshirted the 1985 season). Then the teammates moved to the NBA, where they were both members of the Los Angeles Lakers' 1988 NBA title team.

7. GUS JOHNSON and NATE THURMOND

NBA All-Stars Gus Johnson and Nate Thurmond were high school teammates at Akron Central High in Akron, Ohio in the late 1950s. The future legends played for coach Joe Siegferth, who stressed the importance of defense to his players. Thurmond played center for the team, while Johnson began his career as a 5' 11" guard. Johnson eventually grew to become a 6' 4" high school center. Thurmond became a Hall of Fame center in the pro ranks and a premier rebounding and defensive force. Johnson became a prototypical power forward for the Baltimore Bullets.

8. LAMAR ODOM and CRAIG "SPEEDY" CLAXTON

NBA players Lamar Odom and Craig "Speedy" Claxton were high school teammates at Christ the King High School in New York City. The pair led the team to the city championship game, but eventually lost to Rice. Odom moved to Rhode Island before moving on to the NBA. He has played four seasons for the Los Angeles Clippers and one for the Miami Heat. In the summer of 2004, Odom was traded by the Heat to the Los Angeles Lakers. Claxton starred at Hofstra University before his NBA career began. He has played for the Philadelphia 76ers, the San Antonio Spurs, and the Golden State Warriors.

9. TRENTON HASSELL and SHAWN MARION

NBA players Trenton Hassell and Shawn Marion were teammates at Clarksville High School in Clarksville, Tennessee. In 1996, the pair led their team to a 29–5 record. Marion then went to Vincennes University junior college in Indiana and then to UNLV. He now plays for the NBA's Phoenix Suns, averaging 19 points and more than 9 rebounds per game. Hassell graduated from high school a year after Marion. He stayed in Clarksville to play for Austin Peay University. He then played two years with the Chicago Bulls and now plays for the Minnesota Timberwolves.

10. ADRIAN DANTLEY and KENNY CARR

Adrian Dantley and Kenny Carr were teammates at De-matha High School in Hyattsville, Maryland under legendary coach Morgan Wooten. Dantley graduated in 1973, and Carr a year later in 1974. Dantley starred collegiately at Notre Dame before embarking on a

Austin Peay University

Trenton Hassell.

fifteen-season career in the NBA. Dantley was a seven-time All-Star who averaged better than 30 points per game in four seasons. Carr played college ball at North Carolina State and then played ten seasons in the NBA. Though his career was beset with injuries, Carr still averaged better than 15 points per game in three different seasons.

Charity Kings

*B*asketball's *Most Wanted*™ included a list entitled "Free Throw Woes." The list included players who struggled mightily from the charity stripe. However, the following list contains the opposite—players who were dead-eye marksmen (or women) from the foul line.

1. RICK BARRY

Rick Barry may have been the greatest free throw shooter of all time. His underhanded shot was as accurate as it was distinctive. He led either the ABA or the NBA nine times in his fourteen-year career, including eight of his last ten years. His last three years he led the league with percentages of 92.4, 94.7, and 93.5. His career average was 89.3%.

2. CALVIN MURPHY

Calvin Murphy shot free throws with confidence and it undoubtedly showed in his percentages. In his thirteen-year career, Murphy shot better than 90% for six seasons. In the 1980–81 season he made 206 out of 215 free throws, for an all-time season record of 95.8%. His career free throw average was 89.2%.

3.   MARK PRICE

Mark Price led the NBA in free throw percentage in three of his twelve NBA seasons. In the 1991–92 season, he shot 94.7%, and in the 1992–93 season he shot 94.8%. He was a career 90.4% free throw shooter in the professional ranks.

4.   MAHMOUD ABDUL-RAUF

Mahmoud Abdul-Rauf, formerly Chris Jackson, was a deadeye shot from the free throw line. Twice he led the NBA in free throw percentage. In the 1993–94 season, he shot an amazing 95.6% from the free-throw line, the second-best in NBA history. For his eight-year NBA career, he shot an NBA-best 90.5% from the foul line.

5.   GARY BUCHANAN

Gary Buchanan made 91.3% of his free throws in college, an NCAA record for individuals who made at least 300 free throws in their career. Buchanan made 324 out of 355 for his career at Villanova from 2000 to 2003. In the 2001–02 season as a sophomore, Buchanan set a season record with 71 consecutive free throws made. In that year, he made 97 out of 103 free throws for 94.3%.

6.   CRAIG COLLINS

Penn State's Craig Collins holds the NCAA all-time season free throw percentage mark, for hitting 95.9% of his foul shots during the 1984–85 season. Collins nailed 94 out of 98 free throws during his senior season to set a mark that has yet to be broken.

7. **BILL SHARMAN**

Bill Sharman was a Hall of Fame guard who played all but his rookie season with the Boston Celtics. In his eleven-year career he led the league in free throw percentage seven times. In the 1958–59 season, he nailed 93.2% of his foul shots. He finished his career with an overall average of 88.3%.

8. **LARRY BIRD**

Larry Bird did almost everything well during his stellar thirteen-year career with the Boston Celtics. Foul shooting was no exception, as Bird led the league in free throw percentage in four seasons. In the 1989–90 season he averaged 93% from the line. His career average was 88.6%.

9. **MICHEAL WILLIAMS**

Micheal Williams set an NBA record by making 97 consecutive free throws from March 24, 1993, to November 9, 1993. He was a career 86.8% free throw shooter.

10. **EVA NEMCOVA**

Eva Nemcova merits inclusion on this list for her incredible foul shooting during the 1999 WNBA season with the Cleveland Rockers. In 31 games Nemcova made 62 of 63 free throws, for an astounding 98.4%.

Charismatic Pro Owners

Many times, the public experiences a range of emotions about a charismatic ballplayer, ranging from outrage to admiration. The same feelings can occur toward the owners of ball clubs, particularly if the owner takes a hands-on approach to his or her franchise. The following ten individuals are some highly memorable owners of pro basketball teams.

1. PAT CROCE

Croce's sports career started in the training room and eventually rose to the ownership of an NBA franchise. Croce was a physical therapist with an entrepreneurial mind for sports medicine. He founded Sports Physical Therapists, a sports medicine organization consisting of forty clinics. After selling his company, Croce purchased the lowly Philadelphia 76ers in 1996. With his charisma, work ethic, and never-say-die attitude, Croce built the 76ers into a title-contending franchise.

2. PAT BOONE

The Oakland Oaks only existed for the ABA's first two seasons. Before acquiring the Oaks, basketball junkie

Boone had a team in a Hollywood Studio League that included Bill Cosby and Denny "Tarzan" Miller. Boone lent his name to the Oaks and was awarded 10% of the team—with an agreement indemnifying him from legal responsibility for any debts incurred by the Oaks. Boone was asked to sign a blank check to help out with the team's expenses, and was told that the amount would be around $250,000. The check was actually made out for $1.3 million, and Boone was left holding the bag. But as luck would have it, he was offered $2.5 million to sell and move the team to Washington, D.C., earning back his original investment and then some.

3. FRANKLIN MIEULI

The former owner of the San Francisco (later turned Golden State) Warriors came up with several gimmicks to promote his team and the sport of basketball. Mieuli drafted a female high school player in 1969, and also attempted to start a women's professional league that played before and at halftime of Warriors games. In 1966, he unveiled a new basketball jersey for a road game in New York. The jerseys featured cable cars climbing up the players' backs, including five stars and a picture of the Golden Gate Bridge.

4. MARK CUBAN

The Dallas Mavericks' wealthy owner made it big in the 1990s technology boom, amassing multimillions as the result of two successful startup firms. The first firm, Microsystems, Inc., made millions, and the second, Broadcast.com, made Cuban a billionaire when Yahoo.com purchased it in July 1999. With his earnings from the Broadcast.com sale, Cuban purchased the Dallas Mavericks. As the Mavericks' colorful owner,

Cuban has accumulated more than $1 million in fines for his verbal battles with NBA officials.

5. JACK KENT COOKE

This Los Angeles Lakers owner was an accomplished Canadian high school dropout. Words like flamboyant, generous, and mean have all been used to describe this former Lakers owner, who earned his fortune in the radio industry and became a millionaire by age thirty. Cooke's soap-operatic marital problems also made headlines, with one divorce listed in the 1979 Guinness Book of World Records as the largest divorce settlement up to that time. In 1971, Cooke underwrote the first battle between Muhammad Ali and Joe Frazier, billed as "The Fight of the Century," and sold the closed-circuit viewing rights to theaters worldwide. Cook was also the owner of the NFL's Washington Redskins from 1985 until 1997, and his teams claimed Super Bowls in 1988 and 1992.

6. CHARLIE O. FINLEY

The ABA's Memphis Pros had a miserable 1971-72 season and were on their way out of the league when famed major league baseball owner Charlie O. Finley purchased the franchise and renamed the team. Charlie O. held a contest to rename the franchise, and the winning fan collected $2,500 for the name Tams—the franchise had followers in Tennessee, Arkansas, and Mississippi. Finley named Adolph Rupp as the president of the ball club and changed the team's colors to be similar to the Oakland A's (which he also owned). Finley required mustaches for the players on the Tams and Oakland A's, and he held a "Mustache Promotion" on February 25, 1973, giving away silver mustache spoons to the winners.

7. **GORDON GUND**

Former Cleveland Cavaliers owner Gordon Gund is quite a remarkable person. When Gund and his brother George purchased the Cavaliers in 1983, the team was nicknamed the "Cleveland Cadavers." They were a losing team, averaging about 4,000 fans per game. Since Gund took charge, the Cavs have reached the playoffs ten times in thirteen seasons and average close to 18,000 fans per home game.

In 1970, Gund's vision began to falter, with a progressive degenerative disease of the retina known as Retinitus Pigmentosa (RP) taking what remained of Gordon's vision at age 30. Gund lived the first half of his life with normal vision and the second half in complete darkness, but it hasn't stopped the successful owner from living a successful life. In 2004 Gund sold the team to Dan Gilbert.

8. **JAMES FITZGERALD**

Fitzgerald headed the group that purchased the Milwaukee Bucks franchise in 1976 and produced a young team that won six consecutive division titles with the motto "Green and Growing." Fitzgerald took ownership at a time in the NBA when games weren't broadcast during prime time and many playoff games were recorded to be aired at a later time. Fitzgerald later entered the cable television business to help air more live games, and was chairman of the NBA television committee during some wild and wooly times. Fitzgerald sold the Bucks in 1986 and later purchased the Golden State Warriors

9. **TED TURNER**

A brazen billionaire, Turner was a champion yachtsman and started the Cable News Network (CNN) and

Michael Fitzgerald, Jr.

James Fitzgerald with Bob Lanier.

later Turner Network Television. Turner purchased both the Atlanta Braves and the Atlanta Hawks in 1976, and created the Goodwill Games in 1986. Known as "The Mouth of the South" and "Captain Outrageous" for his brashness, Turner was married to actress-political activist Jane Fonda.

10. JOHN Y. BROWN

The former governor of Kentucky, Brown is truly an accomplished entrepreneur. Brown has previously owned the Kentucky Colonels of the ABA, and later the Buffalo Braves and the Boston Celtics. He governed the state of Kentucky from 1979 to 1983. John Y. also gained notoriety for making fast-food chicken famous in the 1960s as co-owner of Kentucky Fried Chicken, Inc. In 1978, Brown pulled off one of the NBA's greatest business deals, swapping the Buffalo Braves for the Boston Celtics.

Brothers in the NBA

M ore than forty sets of brothers have played basketball in the NBA beginning with Dick and Al Mc-
Guire. They both made Halls of Fame, though Dick
went as a player and Al as a lengendary college coach.
Currently, Jarron and Jason Collins, twins who played
together at Stanford, both play in the NBA. The following are ten sets of basketball-playing brothers who all
played in the NBA.

1. **CALDWELL, CHARLES, MAJOR, and WIL JONES**

No family has put more brothers in the NBA than the
Joneses of McGehee, Arkansas. All four brothers
played college basketball at Albany State in Georgia.
Caldwell was the tallest of the brothers and had, by far,
the most successful career. He played seventeen seasons in the ABA and NBA for six different teams.
Charles Jones played nearly as long from 1983 to 1998
for five teams. Wil was the oldest of the Jones brothers,
and he played in the ABA most of his career. Major
Jones played for six years in the NBA with the Houston
Rockets and the Detroit Pistons.

2. **BRENT, DREW, and JON BARRY**

The Barry boys haven't exactly achieved the all-time great level of their legendary father Rick Barry, who is the only man to win scoring titles in the NCAA, ABA, and NBA, but Jon and Brent have had fine pro careers and are still playing. Brent is the most athletic of the brothers, and won the NBA's dunk contest in 1996. After playing for Oregon State, he played for the Los Angeles Clippers, the Miami Heat, the Chicago Bulls, and the Seattle Supersonics. In the summer of 2004, he was traded to the San Antonio Spurs. Drew Barry played college ball at Georgia Tech before playing in a limited capacity for the Atlanta Hawks, Seattle Supersonics, and Golden State Warriors. Jon also starred for Georgia Tech and has played for seven teams in thirteen NBA seasons.

3. **CAMPY, FRANK, and WALKER RUSSELL**

The Russell brothers all played in the NBA after starring for different college teams in the state of Michigan. Campy, a 6′ 8″ forward, played at the University of Michigan and had the most successful pro career. In the 1978–79 season with the Cleveland Cavaliers, he averaged 21.4 points per game. Frank, the oldest of the three brothers, played college basketball at Detroit. He played only one season (1972–73) with the Chicago Bulls in the NBA. Walker played college ball at Western Michigan. He played professionally in the 1980s with the Detroit Pistons, Atlanta Hawks, and Indiana Pacers.

4. **DICK and TOM VAN ARSDALE**

Dick and Tom Van Arsdale are twins who were both very solid players in the NBA. After playing together at

Indiana University, the brothers both entered the professional ranks in 1965. Dick played for the New York Knicks and the Phoenix Suns. He appeared in three All-Star games and scored more than 15,000 points in his career. For three consecutive seasons, he averaged more than 20 points per game. Tom also played in several All-Star games, though he bounced around to more teams in his career. He scored more than 14,000 points in his career, including two seasons at more than 22 points per game.

5.   **BERNARD and ALBERT KING**

The King brothers were talented small forwards who were excellent shooters. Bernard, the oldest brother, had a Hall of Fame-caliber career in the NBA after stellar play at the University of Tennessee. In ten different seasons he averaged more than 20 points per game, and in the 1984–85 season with the New York Knicks he led the NBA in scoring at 32.9 points per game. He scored nearly 20,000 points in his career. Albert was a high school phenom who had a great career at the University of Maryland. He didn't match his brother's productivity at the professional level however. Albert's best year was his second in the league when he averaged 17 points per game.

6.   **CHUCK and WESLEY PERSON**

The Person brothers both starred at Auburn University and made their mark as perimeter shooters. Chuck, the oldest brother, played in the NBA from 1986 to 2000. In his first seven years in the league, his lowest scoring average was 16.8 points per game. Known as "The Rifleman," he had a memorable shootout with Larry Bird in the playoffs in 1991. Wesley entered the NBA in

1994 and remains an NBA player. Wesley is best known as a three-point specialist. In seven seasons he has averaged better than 40% from behind the arc.

7. DOMINIQUE and GERALD WILKINS

Dominique and Gerald Wilkins are high-flying brothers who played in the NBA for much of the 1980s and 1990s. Dominique, known as "The Human Highlight Film," electrified crowds at the University of Georgia before embarking on a Hall of Fame-caliber career with the Atlanta Hawks. He finished with more than 26,000 career points. Gerald didn't fly quite as high as his brother though he had a respectable career. After playing at the University of Tennessee at Chattanooga, Gerald began playing with the New York Knicks. He averaged as many as 19 points per game in one season. He played for three other NBA teams in a career that spanned from 1985 to 1999.

8. HORACE and HARVEY GRANT

Horace and Harvey Grant are twins who both went to Clemson University after growing up in Georgia. Horace had a great career for the Tigers, but Harvey transferred and eventually played very well for the Oklahoma Sooner team that lost to Kansas and Danny Manning in 1988. Horace played his first seven seasons with the Chicago Bulls. He helped Michael Jordan and Scottie Pippen to the Bulls' first three-peat of championships in the early 1990s. Horace later teamed with Shaquille O'Neal in Orlando to lead the Magic to the championship round, and went on to pick up a ring as a Los Angeles Laker in the 2000–01 season. Harvey was the more slender brother who was known more for his perimeter jumpshot. Harvey had three straight seasons with the Washington Bullets where he averaged better than 18 points per game.

9. JIM and JOHN PAXSON

Jim and John Paxson are brothers who played in the NBA for eleven seasons each, and who are both now general managers of NBA teams. Jim, a 6′ 6″ shooting guard, played in several NBA All-Star games while he was a member of the Portland Trailblazers. He was the general manager for the Cleveland Cavaliers until April 2005. Younger brother John did not garner the individual accolades that his older brother accumulated, but he did obtain something that Jim did not—three championship rings. John often played as the opposing guard to Michael Jordan during the Bulls' first three championships. He sank the series-clinching basket in the 1993 NBA Finals when the Bulls were pressed by a talented Charles Barkley-led Phoenix Suns team. John is now the general manager of the Chicago Bulls.

10. GUS and RAY WILLIAMS

Gus and Ray Williams are high-scoring brothers who played in the NBA in the 1970s and 1980s. Gus had the more high-profile career, as he led the Seattle Supersonics to the NBA championship in 1979. For three straight years in Seattle Williams averaged at least 20 points per game. His brother Ray could also put points on the board, though he never played for a championship team. He averaged better than 20 points per game in two different seasons.

Sibling Teammates in College

Teammates often have special bonds. A select few have even stronger ties because they have the privilege of playing with their sibling. The following are ten sets of siblings who starred together in college:

1. KELLY and COCO MILLER

Kelly and Coco Miller are identical twins who led the University of Georgia to the Final Four and the Elite Eight in back-to-back years. Their efforts led them to share the prestigious 1999 Sullivan Award, given to the nation's top amateur athlete. As seniors, Kelly was named SEC Player of the Year and Coco finished third in the running. Now both sisters play in the WNBA; Kelly plays for the Indiana Fever and Coco plays for the Washington Mystics.

2. PAULA and PAM McGEE

Twin sisters Paula and Pam McGee were teammates and stars at the University of Southern California where they helped lead the Lady Trojans to two consecutive NCAA championships in 1983 and 1984. The dominating duet, who played high school basketball in Michigan, controlled the backboards for USC. Along with Cheryl Miller and Cynthia Cooper, the McGee sisters played on one of the most dominating women's basketball teams ever.

3. ED and CHARLES O'BANNON

Ed and Charles O'Bannon played together on UCLA's 1995 NCAA championship team. Ed, a senior, was the leader of the team, while Charles was a talented underclassman. Ed earned MOP honors in the Final Four, scoring 30 points in the title game. Both brothers played briefly in the NBA. Ed played a total of two seasons with the New Jersey Nets and the Dallas Mavericks. Charles also played two seasons with the Detroit Pistons.

4. JARVIS and JONAS HAYES

Twins Jarvis and Jonas Hayes played together for three years in college. They began their careers at Western Carolina and then transferred to the University of Georgia. The brothers had to split up in 2003 when Jarvis left school a year early to enter the NBA draft, where he was selected by the Washington Wizards.

5. RONELL and DONELL TAYLOR

Ronell and Donell Taylor are called "The Wonder Twins," and they play basketball for the University of Alabama–Birmingham. They attracted the attention of the nation during UAB's stunning upset of top seed Kentucky in the 2004 NCAA tournament. In that game, Ronell stole the ball and threw it behind his head without looking to see who would be on the receiving end of his pass. Donell grabbed the ball and slammed home two key points. "Something in the back of my head said throw it back, somebody's back there," Ronell told reporters. Perhaps it was a special mental connection that he has with his twin brother.

6. JASON and JARRON COLLINS

Twins Jason and Jarron Collins starred at Stanford University together for four years, from 1997 to 2001. The two brothers, standing 6' 11" and 7' tall respectively, dominated the paint for Stanford. They both now play in the NBA; Jason plays for the New Jersey Nets, and Jarron for the Utah Jazz.

7. GIULIANA and GIOCONDA MENDIOLA

Guiliana and Gioconda Mendiola are sister teammates who played for the University of Washington Huskies. The youngest in a family of nine siblings, the Mendiola sisters learned to play basketball by competing against their older brothers. Guiliana was the better player, earning All-American honors. She currently plays for the WNBA's Sacramento Monarchs.

8. DAVID and D.J. HARRISON

David and D.J. Harrison played together at Colorado University in 2002. D.J. played shooting guard and David played center. Their father, Dennis Harrison, played professional football in the NFL. David Harrison played in the NBA in the 2004–05 season for the Indiana Pacers after leaving school following his junior year.

9. ROSCOE and CLIFTON PONDEXTER

Roscoe and Clifton Pondexter are brothers who led Long Beach State in several great seasons in the early

1970s. The pair took a Lute Olsen-coached team to a 24–2 record in 1974, but the Pondexters and the rest of the Long Beach team did not get a chance to play in the NCAA tournament because of team recruiting violations. Clifton played three years in the NBA for the Chicago Bulls, while Roscoe played ten years in Europe and South America. Roscoe's son, Quincy Pondexter, is one of the top young high school basketball players in the country.

10. JON and JOE CRISPIN

Jon and Joe Crispin played together at Penn State, driving opposing defenses crazy with deadly outside shooting. The brothers helped lead Penn State to the 2001 Sweet Sixteen. Joe, the oldest brother, graduated to the NBA where he played one season total with the Los Angeles Lakers and the Phoenix Suns. When his older brother graduated, Jon transferred to UCLA where he was a reserve.

Born on the Same Day

Many people are fascinated with astrology and the twelve signs of the zodiac, reading newspapers and websites daily to find out if their horoscope predicts anything of interest. Some of you trivia buffs with an astrological interest may find this list interesting. It comprises pairs of former and current NBA players who share the same birthday.

1. **DIKEMBE MUTOMBO and WILLIS REED**

Dikembe Mutombo and Willis Reed were both born on June 25. Mutombo, a 7′ 2″ defensive specialist, was born in Kinaisha, Zaire, in 1966. Reed, a 6′ 9″ Hall of Famer, was born in 1942 in Hico, Louisiana.

2. **GARY PAYTON and ANTOINE CARR**

Gary Payton and Antoine Carr were both born on July 23. Payton is a regular on All-Star and All-Defensive teams in his still-active career, and is a lock for the Basketball Hall of Fame. Antoine "Big Dawg" Carr had a fine NBA career in his own right, playing sixteen seasons with the Atlanta Hawks, Sacramento Kings, Utah Jazz, Houston Rockets, and Vancouver Grizzlies.

3. **CLARK KELLOGG, PURVIS SHORT, and LARRY COSTELLO**

Clark Kellogg, Purvis Short, and Larry Costello were all born on July 2. Kellogg was born in Cleveland, Ohio, in 1961; Short was born in 1957 in Hattiesburg, Mississippi; and Costello was born in 1931 in Minoa, New York. Kellogg's career was unfortunately cut short by knee problems, as he was well on his way to becoming a legitimate star in the league. Short was arguably the greatest scorer to never play in a single All-Star game. He had four straight seasons where he averaged more than 20 points per game, including 28 points per game for the Golden State Warriors in the 1984–85 season. Costello played twelve NBA seasons for Philadelphia and Syracuse, and he twice led the league in free throw percentage.

4. **SIDNEY MONCRIEF, ARTIS GILMORE, and DOUG MOE**

Sidney Moncrief, Artis Gilmore, and Doug Moe were all born on September 21. Moncrief was born in Little Rock, Arkansas, in 1957; Gilmore was born in 1948 in Chipley, Florida; and Moe was born in 1938 in Brooklyn, New York. Moncrief was an all-pro guard known for his outstanding leaping ability and defense. Gilmore was a 7′ 2″ intimidating presence with the highest career field goal percentage in NBA history. Moe was a 6′ 5″ forward who starred in the ABA and later became a coach with the Denver Nuggets.

5. **DAN ISSEL, ZELMO BEATY, and DAVE COWENS**

All-star greats Dan Issel, Zelmo Beaty, and Dave Cowens were all born on October 25. Coincidently, all three played center. Issel was born in Batavia, Illinois, in 1948. Cowens was also born in 1948 in Newport, Kentucky. Beaty was born in Hilister, Texas, ten years prior in 1938. Issel scored more than 27,000 points in his ABA and NBA career, and averaged more than 20 points per game in eleven seasons. Beaty was a tough center who averaged more than 20 points per game in five seasons, and who also averaged double figures in rebounds for his career. Cowens was a seven-time All-Star for the Boston Celtics, posting career averages of 17.6 points and 13.6 rebounds.

6. **DARRELL ARMSTRONG, CLYDE DREXLER, and PETE MARAVICH**

Darrell Armstrong, Clyde Drexler, and the legendary "Pistol" Pete Maravich were all born on June 22. Armstrong was born in Gastonia, North Carolina, in 1968; Drexler was born in New Orleans in 1962. Maravich was born in Aliquippa, Pennsylvania, in 1947; and Armstrong is an energizer off the bench who provides instant offense and full-court pressure defense. Drexler was an all-time great who led the Portland Trailblazers to two NBA Finals, and led the Houston Rockets to the NBA title in 1995. Maravich is college basketball's all-time leading scorer, and he also led the NBA in scoring in the 1976–77 season with 31.1 points per game.

7. **BOB McADOO and CHAUNCEY BILLUPS**

Bob McAdoo and Chauncey Billups were both born on September 25. McAdoo, an all-time great, was born in 1951 in Greensboro, North Carolina. He led the NBA in scoring for three straight seasons from 1974 through 1976. Billups was born in 1976 in Denver, Colorado. In the 2004 playoffs, Billups led the Detroit Pistons to an upset win over the Los Angeles Lakers for the championship, and was named series MVP.

8. SLEEPY FLOYD and MICHAEL FINLEY

Eric "Sleepy" Floyd and Michael Finley were both born on March 6. Floyd was born in Gastonia, North Carolina, in 1960; Finley was born in Melrose Park, Illinois, in 1973. Floyd scored more than 12,000 points in thirteen seasons. He is best known for scoring an NBA record 29 points in one quarter in a playoff game. Finley is a star guard who has averaged more than 20 points per game in five straight seasons, and led the league in minutes played in three different seasons.

9. WORLD B. FREE, OTIS BIRDSONG, and CLIFF HAGAN

World B. Free, Otis Birdsong, and Cliff Hagan were all born on December 9. Free was born in 1953 in Atlanta, Georgia; Birdsong was born in Winter Haven, Florida, in 1955; and Hagan was born in Owensboro, Kentucky, in 1931. Free and Birdsong were much better offensive players than defensive players. Free was a playground legend who averaged more than 20 points per game for nine straight seasons. In the 1979–80 season, he tallied 30.2 points per game. Birdsong averaged more than 20 points per game in four seasons, and Hagan was a Hall of Fame-player who scored more than 20 points per game in four *consecutive* seasons.

10. TOM CHAMBERS and DERRICK COLEMAN

Tom Chambers and Derrick Coleman were both born on June 21. Chambers was born in Ogden, Utah, in 1958, while Coleman was born in Mobile, Alabama, in

1967. Chambers scored more than 20,000 points in his NBA career, and in one year he averaged 27.2 points per game. Coleman was a talented player who, for three straight years, averaged more than 20 points and 10 rebounds per game.

Basketball Musicians

Today it seems like many basketball players want to be musicians—and vice versa. There have certainly been numerous high profile athletes who have taken a stab at music, particularly in the rap genre. Likewise, several musicians are serious ballers in their own right and have attempted to play professional basketball.

1. WAYMAN TISDALE

Wayman Tisdale first earned acclaim as an All-America power forward for the University of Oklahoma Sooners. Tisdale played in the NBA from 1986 until 1997 for the Indiana Pacers, Sacramento Kings, and Phoenix Suns. In 1989–90, he averaged 22.3 points per game with the Kings. Tisdale is now known for his skills as a contemporary jazz musician. An accomplished bass player, Tisdale's debut album, *Power Forward*, reached #4 on Billboard's Contemporary Jazz chart. His next album, *In the Zone*, also landed in the top ten on the charts. He has released two other albums: *Decisions* and *Face to Face*.

2. THURL BAILEY

Thurl Bailey was a star forward for the North Carolina State Wolfpack's stunning 1983 NCAA championship team. Bailey starred in the NBA for the Utah Jazz and the Minnesota Timberwolves, and he once tallied 41 points in a 1988 game against the Denver Nuggets. Bailey's passion now is music. He has released three albums: *Faith In Your Heart*, *The Gift of Christmas* and *I'm Not the Same*.

3. PERCY MILLER

Percy Miller is the real name of hip hop legend Master P, a superstar in the rap music industry. He has achieved great success with his label, No Limit Records. Miller is also a hard-core basketball enthusiast and player. He played basketball for the Las Vegas Rattlers of the ABA, the Fort Wayne Fury of the CBA, and other minor league teams. Miller tried out for the NBA's Charlotte Hornets in 1998, and the Toronto Raptors in 1999, but he failed to make either team's final roster.

4. ALLEN IVERSON

Allen Iverson has astonished basketball fans with his amazing accomplishments on the court with both Georgetown University and his current team, the Philadelphia 76ers. Though listed at only 6' 1", which might be generous, the fearless Iverson has led the NBA in scoring three times. He is among the league leaders in steals every season, and he was named the NBA's MVP for the 2000–01 season. Iverson, under the name Jewelz, sought to release a rap album called *Non-Fiction*. It contained the controversial track, *40 Bars*. The song drew cries of protest for its allegedly violent and anti-gay lyrics. Critics of the song included long-time anti-rap activist C. Delores Tucker and NBA commissioner David Stern. The criticism became so intense that the album plans were eventually shelved.

5. SHAQUILLE O'NEAL

The Los Angeles Lakers' Shaquille O'Neal may be the most dominant force the NBA has ever seen. His combination of power, strength, and athleticism make him a true one-of-a-kind player. O'Neal has other interests off the court, including music. He has released six rap albums: *Shaq Diesel*, *Shaq Fu: Da Return*, *You Can't Stop the Reign*, *Respect*, the *Best of Shaquille O'Neal* ,and *Shaquille O'Neal Presents*. . . .

6. WALTER McCARTY

Walter McCarty played a key role for the Boston Celtics as a defensive stopper and spot-up three-point shooter. McCarty starred at the University of Kentucky under then-coach Rick Pitino, but his first love has always been music. In January 2003 he released his debut album, *Moment of Love*, which is marketed as a mix of retro R&B and up-tempo dance music. He now plays for the Phoenix Suns.

7. THOMAS BROOKINS

Thomas Brookins was a former basketball star and jazz musician. He was a star forward for Wendell Phillips High School in Chicago, Illinois, and played semi-pro basketball for the Savoy Big Five, the original version of the Harlem Globetrotters. In 1928, Brookins began performing as a jazz singer for the Original Jimmy Noone's Band. He formed a singing duo with Sammy

Van called Brookins and Van, and died of a stroke in 1988.

8. SID WINGFIELD

Sid Wingfield is a well-known piano and organ blues musician who was recently inducted into the Iowa Blues Hall of Fame. He formed the band Preferred Stock with singer Tony Brown, and has played with such legends as Muddy Waters, Taj Mahal, B. B. King and Albert Collins. Before his career as a professional musician, Wingfield attended the University of North Dakota in the mid 1960s on a basketball scholarship. At North Dakota, he was a teammate of former Los Angeles Lakers coach Phil Jackson.

Harlem Globetrotters

Thomas Brookins, fifth from the left,
in the 1926 Savoy Big Five team photo.

9.   R. KELLY

Pop superstar R. Kelly signed a contract in 1997 to play professional basketball with the Atlantic City Seagulls of the USBL. Apparently, the contract stipulated that Kelly perform the national anthem before several Seagulls games. He loves to play full-court basketball. In fact, basketball was his first love, not music.

10.   CHRIS WEBBER

Chris Webber is an All-Star power forward who plays for the Sacramento Kings. In college, he was a member of the University of Michigan's heralded freshman squad, "The Fab Five," who played two consecutive NCAA championship games. In 1999, Webber released the rap single *Gangsta Gangsta (How U Do It)*, and has also owned an independent record label.

All-Jones Team

M any trivia aficionados like to play name games. Well, here's a list for such readers. All of the following ten NBA players had the same last name of Jones. Apologies may be given to Alvin Jones, Anthony Jones, Askia Jones, Bill Jones, Billy Jones, Casey Jones, Charles Jones, Charles Jones, Charles Jones (see "Same Name" list as to why Charles Jones is listed three times), Collis Jones, Damon Jones . . . well, you get the idea.

In any case, the following ten players were arguably the best players with the name Jones in the history of professional basketball.

1. BOBBY JONES

Bobby Jones was a perennial All-Defensive forward who played the key Sixth Man role for the Philadelphia 76ers' championship team of 1982–83. Beginning in 1977, Jones made eight straight NBA All-Defensive first teams. In 1977–78 he shot 57.8 percent from the field to lead the league.

2. **CALDWELL JONES**

Caldwell Jones was a 6′ 11″ center who played professional basketball for seventeen seasons—five in the
ABA and twelve in the NBA. A tireless defensive presence, Jones led the ABA in blocked shots in his first
season, and averaged double figures in rebounds for
seven seasons in his pro career that included the
ABA & NBA. Jones had three brothers who also played
in the NBA—Major, Charles, and Wil.

3. **K. C. JONES**

K. C. Jones was a talented defensive point guard who
succeeded the great Bob Cousy of the Celtics. Though
he lacked Cousy's flair for the fancy pass, Jones paved
his way to success with a never-say-die attitude. A college teammate of the great Bill Russell at the University
of San Francisco, Jones followed his more-heralded
teammate to the Celtics. Jones became a part of eight
Celtic NBA championships and later coached the team
to two championships in 1984 and 1986.

4. **SAM JONES**

Sam Jones was a great shooting guard for the Boston
Celtics who was a part of ten NBA championship
teams. The master of the bank shot, Jones averaged
as many as 25.9 points per game in a season (1964–
65), and was inducted into the Basketball Hall of Fame
in 1984.

5. **JIMMY JONES**

Jimmy Jones played professional basketball from
1967 to 1977 in the ABA and the NBA. For the first
seven years Jones starred in the ABA with the New

Orleans Buccaneers, Memphis, and the Utah Stars. In his second season with New Orleans, Jones averaged 26.6 points per game. By the time he reached the NBA, at age 30, his best years were behind him.

6. **LARRY JONES**

Larry Jones was a 6′ 2″ gunner who played the majority of his pro career in the ABA. An explosive scorer, Jones averaged more than 21 points per game in his seven seasons in the ABA. In the 1968–69 season with the Denver Nuggets, Jones averaged 28.4 points per game.

7. **EDDIE JONES**

Eddie Jones has been a steady contributor and consistent scorer since he entered the NBA in 1994 for the Los Angeles Lakers. After more than four seasons, Jones moved to the Charlotte Hornets and then to the Miami Heat, where he still plays. His best individual season came in 2000–01, when he led the league in steals and averaged a career-best 20.1 points per game.

8. **STEVE JONES**

Steve "Snapper" Jones is primarily known today as a commentator for NBA games, but Jones was a great player in his own right for the ABA, where he played for seven teams in eight seasons. In two different seasons, Jones averaged more than 20 points per game.

9. **RICH JONES**

Rich Jones was a 6′ 6″, 220-pound forward who played seven seasons in the ABA and one season in the NBA. Jones averaged double figures in scoring in every year of his career. In the 1972–73 season for the Dallas Chapparels, Jones averaged 22.3 points and 10 rebounds per game.

10. **WALI JONES**

Wali Jones was a 6′ 2″ point guard best known as a starter on the great Philadelphia 76ers team of 1966–67—a team that won 68 games and an NBA championship. Jones averaged 13.2 points per game while playing alongside such greats as Wilt Chamberlain, Chet Walker, Hal Greer, and Billy Cunningham.

All-Johnson Team

The last name of Johnson has probably produced the greatest players in the history of professional basketball. More than half the players on this list played in All-Star games. Many won NBA titles. Consider that the following great players all had the same last name.

1. EARVIN "MAGIC" JOHNSON

Earvin "Magic" Johnson was one of the greatest players in NBA history. After leading Michigan State to the NCAA championship in 1979, he moved on to the Los Angeles Lakers and led them to the NBA championship in 1979–80. In the clinching game of the NBA Finals, Johnson scored 42 points and handed out 15 assists. He was a perennial All-Star and NBA leader in assists.

2. GUS JOHNSON

Gus Johnson was a precursor of the modern-day power forward when he played from 1963 to 1973 for the Baltimore Bullets, Indiana Pacers, and Phoenix Suns. The bulk of his career was with the Bullets, where he amassed double figures in points and rebounds on a regular basis. He averaged double figures in rebounds all eight years in the league, including a whopping 17.1 per game in the 1969–70 season.

3. DENNIS JOHNSON

Dennis Johnson was a five-time NBA All-Star who led both the Seattle Supersonics and the Boston Celtics to NBA titles. He was named the MVP of the 1978 NBA Finals for Seattle. Johnson was also named to six first-team All-Defensive squads, and scored more than 15,000 points in his career.

4. KEVIN JOHNSON

Kevin Johnson was one of the best point guards of the late 1980s and 1990s. He regularly averaged nearly 20 points and 10 assists per game. A lethal penetrator, Johnson also possessed an accurate jumper from the perimeter. In three straight seasons from 1988 to 1992, he crossed the magical 20/10 barrier. He retired in the 1999–2000 season with career averages of 17.1 points and 9.1 assists per game.

5. LARRY JOHNSON

Larry Johnson, known by millions for his commercial persona of "Grandmama," dominated college basketball at UNLV. He proceeded to take his inside power game to the Charlotte Hornets, where he formed a dynamic duo with Alonzo Mourning. His best year was his second season in Charlotte, when he averaged 22.1 points and 10.5 rebounds per contest. Leg injuries limited Johnson's lift and effectiveness inside, but he developed a deadly perimeter game with the New York Knicks, helping lead them to the 1999 NBA Finals.

6. MARQUES JOHNSON

Marques Johnson was a classy small forward who posted a career scoring average of more than 20 points per game in his eleven-year NBA career. Johnson played most of his career with the Milwaukee Bucks, where he averaged better than 20 points per game in five seasons.

7. VINNIE JOHNSON

Vinnie Johnson was a bulky 6′ 2″ guard known for his incredible streak shooting. When hot, "The Microwave" was unstoppable. He spent the bulk of his career with the Detroit Pistons, where he played a key role on the "Bad Boys" championship teams of 1988–89 and 1989–90.

8. EDDIE JOHNSON

Eddie Johnson was a sharp-shooting small forward who lasted seventeen years in the NBA. In three different seasons he posted more than 20 points per game, and scored more than 19,000 points in his career.

9. JOHN JOHNSON

John Johnson played twelve seasons in the NBA with little fanfare. He was, however, one of the league's best all-around small forwards. A fine defensive player, Johnson was a member of the Seattle Supersonics' 1978 championship team, along with former Iowa college teammate Freddie Brown.

10. AVERY JOHNSON

Avery Johnson was a 5′ 11″ sparkplug point guard who led the San Antonio Spurs to the NBA title in 1999.

Undrafted out of Southern University, Johnson earned his way into a starting position. Though not a great shooter, the left-handed Johnson was very effective at penetrating and leading a team to victory, and it was these intangibles that separated him from many of his peers.

Academic and Athletic All-Stars

Student athletes sometimes get a bad reputation, as allegations of low academic standards and cheating have surfaced over the years. But the full college experience as a student-athlete requires both brawn and brains. These basketball players performed at an exceptional level in the college classroom, just as they did on the court. They are examples of ideal student-athletes.

1. KERMIT WASHINGTON

Kermit Washington is best known for the devastating punch that he landed on Rudy Tomjonavich when his Los Angeles Lakers were facing the Houston Rockets. Award-winning sportswriter John Feinstein even devoted an entire book, appropriately entitled *The Punch*, to Washington and Tomjonavich. Unfortunately, the dark incident clouded judgment of Washington, who was an outstanding power forward in the NBA.

In college at American University, Washington excelled both on and off the court. He led the nation in rebounding for the 1971–72 and 1972–73 seasons, and in those same two years he was an academic All-American.

2. LOUIE DAMPIER

From 1964 to 1967, Louie Dampier played for the University of Kentucky under legendary coach Adolf Rupp. The great coach once said that Dampier was the best shooter he ever worked with. Dampier tallied 1,575 career points in three seasons playing for Rupp. While at the University of Kentucky, Dampier was an academic All-American for the 1965–66 and 1966–67 school years.

3. DICK VAN ARSDALE

Dick Van Arsdale, along with his brother Tom, starred for the University of Indiana from 1962 until 1965. His senior year, Dick garnered All-America honors for his play and tallied more than 1,200 points in his career. From there he played twelve seasons in the NBA. Van Arsdale excelled in the classroom at Indiana, earning academic All-America honors in 1964 and 1965.

4. ALEC KESSLER

Alec Kessler played for the University of Georgia Bulldogs from 1987 until 1990. He blossomed into an All-Star his senior year, averaging 21 points and more than 10 rebounds per game. He earned SEC Player of the Year for his efforts in leading the Bulldogs to the regular season conference championship, and later played four years in the NBA. Kessler's work in the classroom was especially impressive. He earned a 3.9 grade point average with a major in microbiology at Georgia. He earned academic All-America honors all three years possible (freshman are not eligible) in 1988, 1989 and

1990. Kessler later earned a medical degree from Emory University, and he specializes in orthopedics.

5. MIKE GMINSKI

Mike Gminski tallied more than 2,300 points for the Duke University Blue Devils from 1977 to 1980. In his senior season he averaged more than 21 points and nearly 11 rebounds per game. Gminski then played fourteen seasons in the NBA with the New Jersey Nets, Philadelphia 76ers and Charlotte Hornets. He performed well in the classroom at Duke, a premier academic university, garnering academic All-America honors in 1978, 1979, and 1980.

6. TOM McMILLEN

Tom McMillen starred at the University of Maryland from 1972 to 1974, garnering All-America honors in three straight years. Along with John Lucas and Len Elmore, McMillen helped lead the Terps to the 1972 NIT crown. McMillen played eleven seasons in the NBA for the Buffalo Braves, New York Knicks, Atlanta Hawks, and the Washington Bullets.

McMillen was also an academic All-Star. He was a pre-med major and valedictorian, and he later became the first Rhodes Scholar from the University of Maryland. He earned academic All-America honors in 1972, 1973, and 1974, and he served three terms in the U.S. House of Representatives. McMillen is currently a merchant banker and the chairman of Washington Capital Advisers.

7. MATT BONNER

Matt Bonner starred at the University of Florida from 2001 to 2004, tallying more than 1,400 career points.

Though standing 6' 10", Bonnor was deadly from three-point range. In academics, Bonner was even better. The valedictorian of his high school in New Hampshire, Bonner scored a 1350 on his SAT. He earned academic All-America honors in 2002 and 2003—a year when he was the All-America Member of the Year.

8. DANNY AINGE

Danny Ainge scored 2,467 points for Brigham Young University from 1977 to 1981. In his senior year, 1980–81, he led BYU to the national stage by nailing a last second shot from halfcourt to defeat Notre Dame. He won the John Wooden Player of the Year award his senior year in 1981. An all-around athlete, Ainge played professional baseball with the Toronto Bluejays and is a scratch golfer. Ainge played 14 seasons in the NBA with the Boston Celtics, Sacramento Kings, Phoenix Suns and Portland Trailblazers. He was a member of the 1984 and 1986 Celtic championship teams and played in the NBA finals on several other occasions for both the Suns and the Trailblazers. He coached the Phoenix Suns in 1999 and is now the general manager of the Boston Celtics. Twice, Ainge was named an Academic All-American. He earned a communications degree.

9. ALVAN ADAMS

Alvan Adams played center for the University of Oklahoma from 1973 to 1975, averaging more than 23 points per game and scoring more than 1,700 points in his career. He played twelve seasons in the NBA for the Phoenix Suns, and earned Rookie of the Year honors in 1976. At Oklahoma, he earned academic All-America honors in 1974 and 1975.

10. **PAUL SILAS**

Paul Silas dominated the backboards at the University of Creighton from 1962 to 1964. He led the nation in rebounding in 1963 with more than 20 boards per game. Silas later played sixteen seasons in the NBA, earning three championship rings—two with the Boston Celtics and one with the Seattle Supersonics. Silas earned a bachelor's degree in marketing from Creighton, and in 1964 he was the school's first basketball academic All-American.

Hawkeye Glory

These former basketball stars played at the University of Iowa before moving on to the professional ranks. The list does not include the great Connie Hawkins, who left Iowa during his freshman year without ever playing a game. Hawkins was embroiled in a supposed point-shaving scandal in New York City (the charges were never proven), and he left school to join the Harlem Globetrotters. Iowa has produced many great athletes who later played professional basketball, but these ten achieved great success on the Hawkeye hardwoods.

1. DON NELSON

Don Nelson played at the University of Iowa from 1960 to 1962, leading the team in scoring all three of his varsity seasons. He averaged more than 23 points per game in his junior and senior years, and ended his career with more than 1,500 points to his name. Nelson played fourteen years in the NBA, including stints with the Chicago Zephyrs, the Los Angeles Lakers, and the Boston Celtics, where he won five championships.

After his playing career, Nelson became a coach in the NBA, winning more than 1,000 games. He coached eleven years with the Milwaukee Bucks, seven years with the Golden State Warriors, one year with New York Knicks, and he currently coaches the Dallas Mavericks. He has been named NBA Coach of the Year three times in 1983, 1985, and 1992.

2. FRED BROWN

"Downtown" Freddie Brown became a basketball legend for his ability to drain long jump shots. Brown dialed long distance at Iowa for two seasons, 1969–70 and 1970–71. He averaged 17.9 points per game as a junior and a whopping 27.6 points per game as a senior. Brown left the Hawkeyes for the professional ranks, playing all thirteen of his seasons with the Seattle Supersonics. In 1974, he scored 58 points in a single game. He was part of the Supersonics' 1979 championship team, and the Sonics retired his jersey (#32) in 1986.

3. JOHN JOHNSON

John Johnson may have had an average name, but his basketball game was anything but ordinary. Johnson played for the Hawkeyes for two years, from 1968 to 1970. He scored 1,172 points, including 27.9 per game in the 1969–70 season. Johnson also averaged more than 10 rebounds per game during his college career. After college, Johnson played in the NBA for thirteen years for the Cleveland Cavaliers, the Portland Trailblazers, the Houston Rockets and the Seattle Supersonics. In 1979, he teamed with former college teammate Fred Brown to help the Sonics win their first NBA championship.

4. B. J. ARMSTRONG

Benjamin Roy Armstrong, known as B. J., played for the University of Iowa from 1986 to 1989. He became one of the school's all-time leading scorers and its all-time leader in assists and three-point field goals. Armstrong went on to a stellar career with the Chicago Bulls in the NBA, winning three championship rings. In 1994, he earned his first and only trip to an NBA All-Star game.

5. BOBBY HANSEN

Bobby Hansen starred at Iowa from 1980 to 1984, scoring more than 1,100 points and playing harder than many of his Big Ten competitors. His college coach, Lute Olson, said Hansen's work ethic set him apart from other basketball players. That work ethic enabled Hansen to play nearly a decade in the NBA for the Utah Jazz, Sacramento Kings and the Chicago Bulls. In the 1991–92 season, he played for the Bulls' championship team, and in the clinching game of the NBA Finals against the Portland Trailblazers, Hansen sparked the team's dramatic fourth-quarter comeback.

6. KEVIN KUNNERT

Kevin Kunnert starred at Iowa from 1970 to 1973, leading the team in rebounding for three straight years. In 1972, he averaged nearly 15 rebounds per game. The 7-footer remains the Hawkeyes all-time leading rebounder. Kunnert could also score in the college game. In his senior season in 1973, he averaged more than 19 points per game. Kunnert moved to the professional ranks, playing 9 seasons with the Buffalo Braves, the Houston Rockets, the San Diego Clippers and the Portland Trailblazers.

7. GERRY WRIGHT

Gerry Wright was not the greatest scorer or rebounder in Hawkeye history; he does not rank among the leaders in other statistical categories; he wasn't even the best player on any of the Iowa teams of the late 1980s when he played. However, Wright deserves mention in this list for his high-wire act on the court. His aerial attack earned him the nickname "Sir Jamalot." Wright earned his undergraduate and master's degrees from Iowa, and though he was drafted by the Detroit Pistons, he joined the Navy instead. Wright is now a published author, having written *Straight Talk*, a book about relationships.

8. ROY MARBLE

Roy Marble scored more than 2,000 points in his illustrious career for the Hawkeyes from 1985 to 1989. In his senior season, he averaged more than 20 points per game. An athletic 6' 6" guard and forward, Marble drew comparisons to Clyde Drexler and Michael Jordan. Unfortunately, Marble's professional career did not live up to the hype. He played only 29 NBA games in two seasons, but when he played for the Hawkeyes, Marble was often the best player on the court.

9. ED HORTON

Ed Horton played at Iowa from 1985 to 1989, along with fellow star Roy Marble. Horton was a rugged rebounder and fierce competitor who scored nearly 1,400 points in his four-year college career. In his senior season, he blossomed as a scorer, tallying more than 18 points per game. Like Marble, Horton's NBA career was short-lived. He played 45 games for the

Washington Bullets in the 1989–90 season, and never played again in the NBA.

10.   RICKY DAVIS

Ricky Davis played only one year for the University of Iowa before he took his tremendous athletic ability to the NBA. In the 1998 season, Davis led the team in scoring with 15 points per game. Davis has played for four teams in his eight-year NBA career, including the Charlotte Hornets, the Miami Heat, the Cleveland Cavaliers and the Boston Celtics. He continues to dazzle with his amazing skills but is best known for his selfish attitude.

Famous Quotes

B asketball history has been blessed with some of the most memorable characters of all time. It has also been blessed with some great sayings that have transcended the sports world. The following ten quotes have crossed over from basketball into other aspects of culture.

1. **"DON'T EVER GIVE UP"**

Former North Carolina State University basketball coach, Jim Valvano uttered these words in his memorable acceptance speech for the ESPY's inaugural Arthur Ashe Courage and Humanitarian Award in 1993. Valvano, whose Wolfpack won the NCAA title as heavy underdogs in 1983, was battling terminal cancer at the time of the stirring speech. "Cancer can take away all my physical abilities," he said. "It cannot touch my mind, it cannot touch my heart and it cannot touch my soul." The Jimmy V Foundation for Cancer Research continues as a lasting tribute to the beloved coach.

2. "THE OPERA AIN'T OVER 'TIL THE FAT LADY SINGS"

Texas-based sports broadcaster and writer, Dan Cook used the phrase after a playoff game between the San Antonio Spurs and the Washington Bullets in 1978. Cook used the phrase apparently in reference to operas that often conclude with a well-sized soprano. Cook's saying was apt because the Bullets came back from a Game 1 defeat to win the series, and later the NBA title. Bullets coach Dick Motta also used the phrase several times, including when his Bullets trailed the Seattle Supersonics 2–1 in the NBA Finals in 1978. His statement was prescient because the Bullets—led by Wes Unseld and Elvin Hayes—finally captured the crown. Interestingly, the quote is usually attributed to Motta rather than Cook.

3. "THE SHIP BE SINKIN'"

The talented but troubled guard, Michael Ray Richardson, uttered his classic phrase after his New York Knicks won only 33 games in the 1981–82 season. The previous year, the Knicks had won 50 games. The team traded Richardson to Golden State, which then traded him shortly thereafter to the New Jersey Nets. Richardson was a great talent who led the league in steals three times; however, his own NBA career sank in 1986 when he became the first player in league history to be banned under the NBA's three-strikes drug policy. Richardson rebuilt his life while playing basketball overseas. He retired from basketball at the age of 46, and returned to the NBA in 2003 as a community ambassador for the Denver Nuggets.

4. "I AM NOT A ROLE MODEL"

Superstar forward Charles Barkley uttered this classic phrase several times, including for a well-publicized, 1993 commercial for Nike shoes. Barkley insisted that parents, not athletes, should be role models for kids. For much of his illustrious career, Barkley was indeed not a role model. He was accused of spitting on a fan, throwing a man through a window at a Milwaukee bar, and elbowing a player from Angola during the Olympics. Whatever his stance on role models, Barkley has become one in terms of excellence—from his Hall of Fame career to his status as one of the best commentators for the NBA.

5. "NOBODY ROOTS FOR GOLIATH"

NBA goliath Wilt Chamberlain often said this to reporters after an away game in which he was the object of boos from opposing crowds. Chamberlain was a dominant force in the NBA: He averaged more than 50 points per game in one season, led the league in assists one year as a center, averaged an astonishing 24 rebounds per game in one season, and tallied 100 points in a single game. Many of his records will never be broken.

6. "I THINK IT'S JUST GOD DISGUISED AS MICHAEL JORDAN"

Boston Celtics great Larry Bird uttered these words after watching Michael Jordan torch his team for 63 points during an April 20, 1986, playoff game. Jordan nearly led his team to a victory that day in the Boston Garden. Despite Jordan's individual glory, the Celtics prevailed 135–131 in double overtime. They swept the

Bulls 3–0 after capturing the next game. Jordan would have to wait until 1991 before winning his first championship.

7. "FO, FO, FO"

Moses Malone gave this pithy but nearly prophetic statement about how his Philadelphia 76ers would fare during the 1983 playoffs. Malone predicted his team would win four straight in all three rounds before clinching the championship. The 76ers, led by Malone and Julius Erving, nearly accomplished the remarkable feat by sweeping the New York Knicks. The 76ers then beat the Bucks 4–1 in the Eastern conference finals. In the championship round, Malone revised his prediction to "Fo, Fi, Fo." Malone was right, as the 76ers swept the Los Angeles Lakers to win the title.

8. "ALL RIGHT, WHO'S PLAYING FOR SECOND PLACE?"

Larry Bird, a notorious trash talker, made this confident statement in the locker room before the NBA's inaugural Long Distance Shootout competition at the 1986 All-Star weekend in Dallas. The competition featured such premier marksmen as Dale Ellis, Craig Hodges, and Trent Tucker. However, Bird saw them as no threat to his crown. Bird backed up his trash talk and defeated Hodges 22–12 in the final round. Bird won the competition all three years he was entered. Ironically, Hodges later won the competition three times as well—but he couldn't do it when Larry Bird was his competitor.

9. "WE'RE TALKING ABOUT PRACTICE"

Allen Iverson, the Philadelphia 76ers' star guard, uttered his famous "practice" comments during a May

2002 press conference after the Sixers had been eliminated from the playoffs. Iverson was often criticized by his then coach Larry Brown for failing to perform or attend practices on a regular basis. In response to a reporter's question about missing practices, Iverson responded:

> Now I know that I'm supposed to lead by example and all that but I'm not shoving that aside like it don't mean anything. I know it's important, I honestly do but we're talking about practice. We're talking about practice man. [laughter from the media crowd] We're talking about practice. We're talking about practice. We're not talking about the game. We're talking about practice.

Some view this infamous interview as the epitome of Iverson's me-first, non-team approach. Others counter that Iverson plays as hard as anyone else in actual games, and he regularly plays hurt. Iverson has won three scoring titles and earned MVP honors in 2001.

10. "ASK NOT WHAT YOUR TEAMMATES CAN DO FOR YOU. ASK WHAT YOU CAN DO FOR YOUR TEAMMATES."

Taking a cue from former President John F. Kennedy's classic "Ask not what your country can do for you, but what you can do for your country," Los Angeles Laker great Earvin "Magic" Johnson altered the phrase to involve basketball teammates. This saying epitomized Johnson's career as he helped turn the Lakers into world champs in his rookie season.

The Best of
Al McGuire

A l McGuire was a unique, confident, and street-savvy coach who led the Marquette Warriors to a 1977 NCAA basketball title, and later became a popular basketball analyst. McGuire was known for his quick Irish wit and charming charisma. Listed below are ten of his memorable sayings:

1. ON HIS SHORT NBA CAREER

"I stayed in the league [NBA] three years by diving over press tables and starting fights." McGuire played three years as a reserve in the NBA for the New York Knicks and was noted more for his hustle and ambition than for his skill level.

2. ON CATHOLIC SCHOOLS

"You can always tell the Catholic schools by the length of the cheerleaders skirts."

Al McGuire, a lifelong Catholic, often liked to joke about the longer length of the skirts of opposing cheerleaders at other Catholic universities.

3. ON SCREAMING

"But coaching college is not pizza parties and getting the team together at the A&W stand. People can't understand my players screaming back at me, but it's healthy. Also, I notice that the screaming always comes when we're 15, 20 ahead. When it's tied, they're all listening very carefully to what I have to say." This was an explanation from McGuire about how he had the respect of his team, even when his players voiced their opinions.

4. ON HANK RAYMOND

"Hank's a perfectionist. I've always said, if he were married to Raquel Welch, he'd expect her to cook." Al McGuire left the practices and details of his Marquette teams in the hands of his assistant coach, Hank Raymonds. Raymonds was an organized assistant that handled the X's and O's, and McGuire was the visionary that showed up on game day to lead the charge. Raymond later succeeded McGuire as coach of Marquette.

5. ON RECRUITING

"My rule was I wouldn't recruit a kid if he had grass in front of his house. That's not my world. My world was a cracked sidewalk." McGuire, a native of New York, had a reputation for bonding with inner-city players.

6. ON MICROPHONE TROUBLES

"I've had more dead mikes than an Irish funeral." Coach McGuire was proud of his Irish roots and often liked to include his heritage in his humor.

Marquette University Archives

Al McGuire, legendary coach and announcer.

7. ON EDUCATION

"I think everyone should go to college and get a degree and then spend six months as a bartender and six months as a cab driver. Then we would really be educated." Al was known for his street smarts and always thought a person could improve their knowledge of the world and complete their education by mixing with all walks of life.

8. ON RECRUITING STAR PLAYER BUTCH LEE

"There were some three hundred schools after Butch Lee, and he narrowed it down to Marquette and Penn. Butch lived in Harlem, and I visited his place once. I told him that freshmen weren't [at that time] eligible in the Ivy League, so if he went to Penn, his first year he'd be playing games at 5:30 on the third floor of some YMCA against guys who dribble with two hands and have their underwear hanging out of their uniforms. But come to Marquette and you'll play before packed houses and on national TV. It's Park Avenue compared to Brownstone walk-up." McGuire used the term, "Park Avenue" when referring to something that was high class, and he used it to recruit his 1977 championship team star, Butch Lee, to Marquette.

9. ON TIMING

"I need to make the phone ring, so I'm getting in the tub." McGuire thought that timing could mean everything to getting a deal done. While recruiting, Al used to joke about what it took to make the phone ring to get things happening.

10. ON LIFE AS TV ANALYST

"A person like me just burns himself out. We color commentators aren't qualified, we're just passing through, like Elizabeth Taylor in a nightgown, or a watermelon in a boa constrictor. But it's a nice ego trip and exciting to be picked up by a limousine." McGuire enjoyed his years as a television analyst, but he realized he earned his job from his success as a coach and his charismatic personality.

Asian Invasion

B asketball is now a global game, and the NBA has witnessed a dramatic increase in the number of international players in the league. Basketball is an extremely popular sport in many areas of the world, including the Far East. The following players have come from Asia to make an impact in the basketball world.

1. YAO MING

Ming was the first draft pick for the 2002–03 NBA season and is one of the Houston Rockets' top players. His extreme popularity in the league garnered him enough votes to win the starting center position for the Western Conference team during the 2004 and 2005 All-Star games. Before coming to the Rockets, Ming had a successful professional basketball career with the Shanghai Sharks of the Chinese Basketball Association and the national Chinese basketball team.

2. MA JIAN

Jian played at the University of Utah before being the last player cut by the Los Angeles Clippers at the end of the 1996 training camp. Jian, an effective ball-handler, tried out in the United States following a dispute with Chinese basketball officials. After failing to make the Clippers, Jian returned to play professional basketball in China.

3. SONG TAO

Tao was chosen by the Atlanta Hawks in the third round of the 1987 NBA draft, after starring as a center for the Chinese national team. The 6′ 10″ Song signed a one-year contract worth a reported $70,000 but did not make it to the season opener after suffering a knee injury during the NBA exhibition opener.

4. WANG ZHIZHI

The 7′ 1″ Zhizhi, who became the first Chinese player in the NBA, starred on the 1996 and 2000 Chinese Olympic teams. Wang's 2000 Olympic team troubled the USA team in the early going until foul trouble set in. Wang led his Chinese Basketball Association team, the Bayi Rockets, to six consecutive national championships before Don Nelson and the Dallas Mavericks decided to draft him with their 2nd round pick in the 1999 NBA draft.

5. ZHENG HAIXIA

At 6′ 8″ and 254 pounds, Chinese female basketball center Zheng Haixia became a professional baskeball player in the United States when she was drafted by the Los Angeles Sparks of the WNBA in the second round in 1996.

6. WATARU MISAKA

Misaka is the first Asian to play in the NBA. The 5′ 7″ Japanese-American guard played three games with the 1947–48 New York Knicks. Misaka was born in Ogden, Utah and played college ball for nearby Weber State, and later the University of Utah, leading the Utes to the 1944 NCAA championship.

7. RI MYONG HUN

Hun, also known as Michael Ri after his hero Michael Jordan, hails from North Korea and is the tallest basketball player in the world. Ri first attracted international attention when he appeared in the 1990 Asian Games in Beijing, thus creating an interest in several NBA teams hoping to sign the giant 7′ 9″ center as a free agent. However, unfavorable diplomatic relations between North Korea and the United States prevented Ri from entering the country and joining the NBA. Ri fell victim to a law known as the Trading With the Enemy Act. The act bans companies in the United States from forming business relations with North Korea.

8. MENGKE BATEER

The Denver Nuggets signed Mengke Bateer on February 26, 2002, as a free agent. He had previously played for the Beijing Ducks of the Chinese Basketball Association, and starred as center for the 1996 and 2000 Chinese Olympic teams. Approximately 400 million people in China tuned in when Bateer's Denver Nuggets faced Wang Zhizhi's Dallas Mavericks on March 3, 2002.

9. HU WEIDONG

Weidong, who was the 1999 MVP of the Asian Championships, was offered a ten-day contract with the Atlanta Hawks in 2000. The opportunity never materialized for

Hu, though. He was injured while practicing with the Chinese national team, and wasn't able to begin his NBA tryout.

10. YUTA TABUSE

Yuta Tabuse, a point guard from Japan, led Noshiro Kogyo High School to three consecutive national titles and played college ball at BYU-Hawaii. He also played with the Dallas Mavericks in 2002 Summer League and was invited to the Denver Nuggets training camp in 2003. He played in three games during the preseason, averaging 3 points per game, but was cut before the 2003 season, ending his bid to become the first Japanese-born NBA player.

Globetrotter Favorites

A colorful, charismatic promoter named Abe Saperstein created a pioneering basketball team called the Savoy Big Five. This team evolved into the Chicago-based Harlem Globetrotters, a team that traveled the nation defeating all kinds of teams and thrilling fans with crowd-pleasing theatrics. The following ten are some of the Globetrotters' most popular players.

1. CONNIE HAWKINS

Hawkins was a tremendous ball handler who played four seasons with the Globetrotters in the mid-1960s. After his stint with the Globetrotters, Hawkins went on to star in the ABA, leading the Pittsburgh Pipers to the first ABA title and claiming the league's MVP for the year. Hawkins later spent seven years in the NBA and was inducted into the Basketball Hall of Fame in 1992.

2. WILT CHAMBERLAIN

Chamberlain was the greatest player in the history of the Harlem Globetrotters. He began his professional basketball career in 1958 when he signed one of sports' largest contracts with the Globetrotters. Wilt was a member of the first Globetrotter team to play in Russia in 1959. After playing a year with Harlem, he signed on with the NBA and became one of history's most dominant centers. Wilt was honored a year after his death in 2000, when his jersey became the first one ever retired by the Globetrotters.

3. REECE "GOOSE" TATUM

Goose first played with the Globetrotters in 1941, but he was soon drafted into the Air Force in World War II. After finishing his tour, Tatum came back to the Globe-trotters for ten more years (1946–56). He was one of the funniest Globetrotters in the history of the organiza-tion. Tatum liked being a clown and said, "My goal in life is to make people laugh." Some of Tatum's favorite antics included, using a trick basketball and fooling with the referees. He developed many of the team's co-medic routines.

4. HUBERT "GEESE" AUSBIE

Ausbie attended Philander Smith College in Little Rock, Arkansas, where he was the third highest scorer in col-lege basketball nationwide. Geese signed on with the Globetrotters in 1961, playing more than 10,000 games in more than 100 nations, including all fifty state capitals. Ausbie was the chief showman for the Globe-trotters from 1961 to 1988, before coaching the organi-zation.

5. LYNETTE WOODARD

Lynette Woodard, one of the greatest women's college basketball players of all time, donned the Globetrotters uniform for the first time on November 13, 1985, in

Spokane, Washington. She was the first woman ever to play for the Globetrotters.

6. MARQUES HAYNES

Haynes, considered the greatest dribbler in basketball history, had two stints with the Harlem Globetrotters (1947 to 1953 and 1972 to 1979). Haynes starred in college at Langston University, leading his school to a 112–3 record, which included a 59-game winning streak. Haynes grabbed the eye of Globetrotter owner Abe Saperstein, following Langston University's victory over the Globetrotters. After college, Marques joined Harlem and assisted them in a huge victory over George Mikan's Minneapolis Lakers in 1948.

7. FRED "CURLEY" NEAL

Known for his sharp wit and bald dome, Neal was a gifted shooter and dribbler and was famous for consistently sinking half court shots. Neal played college hoops at Johnson C. Smith University in Charlotte, N.C., averaging 23.1 points per game, before going on to play twenty-two years as one of the most beloved Globetrotters of all time.

8. MEADOWLARK LEMON

Lemon was known as the "Clown Prince" of basketball, for his fun-filled antics and exuberant personality. While starring for the Harlem Globetrotters for twenty-four seasons, Lemon compiled a streak of more than 7,500 consecutive games. In the spring of 1952, Meadowlark sent the Globetrotters a letter asking for a try-out. Meadowlark's first season in professional basketball was with the Kansas City Stars, a developmental team of the Globetrotters, but he soon moved up to the Harlem team in 1954.

9. **"SWEET LOU" DUNBAR**

Dunbar played for the University of Houston in the early 1970s. Sweet Lou averaged 23 points on his way to earning All-America honors. Dunbar was drafted in 1975 by the ABA's San Diego Conquistadors and played professional basketball in Switzerland before joining the Globetrotters in 1976. Dunbar is one of the all-time funny men in Globetrotter history, and he is now in his twenty-sixth year with the organization.

10. **CURLEY "BOO" JOHNSON**

Johnson played college basketball for Loras College Duhawks in Dubuque, Iowa. Boo became the first Duhawk to have his jersey retired at Loras. Johnson has been with the Globetrotters for sixteen seasons, and his ball-handling antics make him a close second to the great Marques Haynes. Boo has performed on every continent and in more than 70 countries for the Globetrotters.

Harlem Globetrotters

Curley "Boo" Johnson.

Best Basketball Movies

L ike several other sports, basketball has fared quite
well in cinema with many classic films. The following are ten of the best:

1. *HOOSIERS*

Gene Hackman stars as tough high-school coach Norman Dale in this critically acclaimed 1986 movie. The
movie is loosely based on Indiana's tiny Milan High
School basketball team, which played its way to an
upset in a dramatic state high school championship
under coach Marvin Wood. Dennis Hopper stars as the
town's basketball-loving drunk, Shooter, and gives a
memorable performance for which he earned an Academy Award best supporting actor nomination.

2. *HOOP DREAMS*

At the time, *Hoop Dreams* was the highest-grossing
documentary in history, starring high school basketball
stars William Gates and Arthur Agee. The 1994 film
chronicles these two hoopsters' pursuit of basketball
scholarships to Catholic high schools, and their goal of

playing in the pros like their hero, Isiah Thomas. The three-hour documentary provides an insight into the high school and college recruitment process. Cameos include Bobby Knight, Isiah Thomas, and Dick Vitale. The film received an Academy Award nomination for Best Film Editing but, surprisingly, did not receive a nomination for best documentary.

3. *ONE ON ONE*

Robbie Benson plays naive, small town basketball player Henry Steele who is recruited to a college in Colorado. Benson's character soon finds out that athletic ability alone is not the only quality a basketball player needs to succeed, as he deals with a sadistic coach who seems to be hell-bent on making Steele quit the team.

4. *FAST BREAK*

Gabe Kaplan of *Welcome Back Kotter* fame stars as David Greene, the head coach of a struggling Nevada college basketball team. Former NBA players Bernard King and Mike Warren also co-star. Greene heads to the Big Apple to recruit new talent—one of which is a female disguised as a male—in this entertaining movie. Look for Laurence Fishburne in a small role as a street kid.

5. *MAURIE*

The 1973 drama is based on the life of Cincinnati Royals star Maurice Stokes, who earned the 1958 Rookie of the Year Award. Stokes's NBA career was cut short by a freak head injury that led to paralysis. Stokes's teammate, Jack Twyman, dedicated his life to helping his fallen friend and became Maurice's legal guardian.

6. *HE GOT GAME*

Denzel Washington stars as the father of highly-recruited New York High School star Jesus Shuttlesworth, played by NBA star Ray Allen. Washington plays an ex-con trying to inspire his son to play basketball. The 1998 Spike Lee film highlights the father/son relationship of Allen and Washington, and the pressures placed on hopeful athletes. Lee apparently wanted Allen Iverson to play the lead character, but Iverson turned him down. The movie also includes a cameo by Michael Jordan.

7. *WHITE MEN CAN'T JUMP*

This fast-paced, 1992 comedy starring Wesley Snipes and Woody Harrelson is entertaining and includes a lot of in-your-face street dialogue. It is about the life of two basketball hustlers trying to make it in a cut throat business. Look for a cameo by Laker announcer Chick Hearn. Several former NBA players also have cameos, including former All-Star Marques Johnson.

8. *GO, MAN, GO*

This 1954 film starring Dane Clark and Sidney Poitier is based on the history and development of the Harlem Globetrotters, and was one of the few films directed by famed cinematographer James Wong Howe. Clark plays Globetrotter founder Abe Saperstein.

9. *REBOUND*

James Earl Jones stars in this 1996 film about the true story of the Harlem playground legend Earl "The Goat" Manigault, who ruined his chance at a NBA career with drugs. Manigault, whom Kareem Abdul-Jabbar once called the best player he ever saw, later sobers up to help others by running an inner-city program for drugs. Abdul-Jabbar appears in a small cameo in the film.

10. *INSIDE MOVES*

Basketball is the backdrop in this overlooked 1980 film about a group of misfits at a San Francisco tavern called Max's. The bartender, played by David Morse, receives an offer to play for the Golden State Warriors. It is a drama that covers attempted suicide, drug use, prostitution, and NBA life in the Bay Area. Watch for Robert Parish and Jo Jo White in cameo appearances.

Worst Basketball Movies

Not all cinematic creations that feature Dr. Naismith's sport are classics. In fact, some might well be classified as "bricks." Suffice it to say, the following ten movies did not come close to winning any Academy Awards.

1. *THE FISH THAT SAVED PITTSBURGH*

This 1979 movie features the lowly Pittsburgh Pythons who struggle to the worst record in the NBA, until an astrologer turns the team around by suggesting they use only players who are Pisces—the same sign as star player Moses Guthrie, played by Julius Erving. The team transforms itself into the winning Pittsburgh Pisces. The plot is absurd and viewers are subjected to a steady steam of disco music. The film's only redeeming quality is some of the basketball action, featuring the high-flying Erving, Meadowlark Lemon, and Kareem Abdul-Jabbar.

2. *JUWANNA MANN*

The premise for this regrettable farce is *Tootsie* on the basketball court. A failed NBA star, played by actor

Miguel Nunez, makes his return to professional basketball as a woman in the female pro league. Unbelievably, Nunez pursues the team's captain, played by the beautiful Vivica A. Fox. Unlike Dustin Hoffman's *Tootsie*, this 2002 movie garnered no Academy Award nominations.

3. *CELTIC PRIDE*

This awful 1996 movie featured Dan Aykroyd and Daniel Stern as obsessed Boston Celtics fans who kidnap the star player of the Los Angeles Lakers, played by Damon Wayans. Famous movie critic Leonard Maltin rates this movie as a "BOMB." No argument here.

4. *COACH*

Cathy Lee Crosby stars as the surprise coach of a boys' high school basketball team who scores big with at least one of her players. Unfortunately, the action on the court is overshadowed by Crosby's Mrs. Robinson-esque exploits.

5. *PORKY'S REVENGE*

It is sad how *Porky's II: The Next Day* and *Porky's Revenge* ruined a series that started out fairly well with the first *Porky's* movie. The third and final movie, *Porky's Revenge* (1985), features the gang as stars on the Angel Beach High basketball team, who have to decide whether to throw the state championship.

6. *SLAM DUNK ERNEST*

Jim Varney stars in yet another *Ernest* movie. In this 1995 film, Ernest P. Worrell is a terrible benchwarmer until a pair of magical shoes transform him into a star. This ridiculous plot will be enjoyed only by fans of the

Ernest series. Kareem Abdul-Jabbar also has a role in the film.

7. *AIR BUD*

Air Bud may tickle the fancy of very young kids, but the plot shows why this movie deserves mention on the list. A new kid in town befriends a dog who has an uncanny ability to shoot basketball. Enough said about this 1997 film.

8. *TEEN WOLF TOO*

Teen Wolf Too does the impossible: it makes the original *Teen Wolf* movie look good. The 1987 sequel stars Jason Bateman instead of Michael J. Fox, which is one of its flaws. Bateman plays Fox's cousin who goes to college on a basketball scholarship. He, like Fox's character, plays great basketball when he turns into a wolf. Movie critic Leonard Maltin rates this movie a "BOMB" and rightfully calls it "excruciating."

9. *LIKE MIKE*

This well-meaning 2002 story features rapper Lil' Bow Wow as orphan Calvin Cambridge, a kid who becomes an NBA star with his magical shoes. The sight of Lil' Bow Wow going head-to-head with NBA stars like Allen Iverson may capture kids' imaginations, but it certainly won't win any cinematic awards. Lil' Bow Wow is a much better rapper than actor.

10. *BASEketBALL*

This ridiculous 1998 comedy features two guys who invent their own game of blacktop basketball—a combination of baseball and basketball. Directed by David Zucker, the movie stars *South Park* creators Trey Parker and Matt Stone, who should have stuck to what made them famous.

High School 100-Point Scorers

On March 2, 1962, the Philadelphia Warriors' Wilt Chamberlain did the impossible: he scored 100 points in a single game. He never scored 100 points in a high school game while at Overbrook High School in Philadelphia. But the following ten players did score 100 points or more in a high school game.

1. LISA LESLIE

On February 7, 1990, Lisa Leslie scored 101 points for Morningside High in Inglewood, California—in a single half. Morningside was ahead 102–24 over South Torrance at halftime when South Torrance refused to take the court for the second half. Leslie scored 49 points in the first quarter and 52 points in the second quarter, and is now a star in the WNBA with the Los Angeles Sparks.

2. CHERYL MILLER

On January 26, 1982, Cheryl Miller scored 105 points, and her team Riverside Poly defeated Riverside Norte Viste 179–15. Miller later starred and coached at the

University of Southern California. Coincidentally, as a coach, one of Miller's star players was none other than Lisa Leslie.

3. JEANETTE HAYS

On January 6, 1956, Jeanette Hays of Henry, Tennessee, scored 100 points in a high school basketball game.

4. PETE CIMINO

On January 22, 1960, Pete Cimino scored 114 points for Bristol High School in their 132–86 win over Palisades. Cimino made 44 of 79 attempts from the floor, and 26 of 29 free throws.

5. DANNY HEATER

On January 26, 1960, Danny Heater scored an incredible 135 points for Burnsville High School in its 173–43 victory over Widen. Heater scored 55 points in the first half and 80 points in the second half, adding 32 rebounds and 7 assists.

6. DAJUAN WAGNER

On January 16, 2001, Dajuan Wagner scored 100 points for Camden High in their 157–67 win over Gloucester Township Technical School. Wagner, the son of former Louisville great and NBA player Milt Wagner, shot 42 of 61 from the field, including 10 three-pointers.

7. DENISE LONG

On January 23, 1968, Denise Long scored 111 points in a high school game for Union Witten High School in Union Whitten, Iowa. Long scored more than 100 points three times in her legendary career. She was so good that the San Francisco Warriors of the NBA drafted her. Unfortunately, she never played.

8. LYNEE LORENZEN

In 1986, Lynne Lorenzen scored 100 points in a game for Ventura High in a win over Woden-Crystal Lake. She averaged better than 60 points per game her senior year and scored a whopping 6,736 points in her high school career.

9. DICK BOGENRIFE

On February 6, 1953, Dick Bogenrife of Sedalia High School in Midway, Ohio, scored 120 points in a single high school basketball game. Sedalia defeated Canaan 137–46. Bogenrife scored 52 field goals and 16 free throws to amass his amazing total.

10. NORMA SCHOULTE

On January 28, 1952, Norma Schoulte scored 111 points to lead Monona High School in Monona, Louisiana, to a lopsided tournament win over Harpers Ferry. Schoulte scored 4,187 points in her high school basketball career from 1948 to 1952.

Draft Oddities

For the past few years, the NBA draft has been limited two two rounds, so teams must be very careful about whom they select. For years though, the NBA had a draft that went into numerous rounds, which explains why there have been some rather odd draft selections in the past. The following ten qualify as unusual draft selections.

1. DAVE WINFIELD

Winfield is the only athlete in sports history to be drafted by four professional teams in three sports—baseball's San Diego Padres, football's Minnesota Vikings, the NBA's Atlanta Hawks, and the ABA's Utah Stars. He chose baseball as his profession and it was probably a wise choice. Winfield was selected to the All-Star team twelve times, earned seven Gold Glove Awards, smacked more than 3,000 base hits, and was inducted into the Hall of Fame in his first year of eligibility in 2001.

2. JIM BROWN

The legendary running back Brown averaged 104.3 yards per game in his NFL career. After playing only nine seasons in the NFL, Brown became the league's all-time rusher—at a time when the regular season was only twelve games compared to the sixteen it is today. Jim was a tremendous athlete at Syracuse University and also starred on the basketball team. The local professional basketball team, the Syracuse Nationals, drafted Brown in the ninth round of the 1957 draft.

3. BRUCE JENNER

Jenner was labeled the "World's Greatest Athlete" after winning the decathlon in the 1976 Olympic Games in Montreal. The Kansas City Kings took the best available athlete in the seventh round of the NBA draft in 1977.

4. TONY GWYNN

A former eight-time National League batting champion with San Diego Padres, Gwynn played baseball and basketball at San Diego State University and left the school holding the all-time record in assists. Tony was drafted in 10th round by San Diego Clippers in the 1981 NBA draft. Gwynn is now the head baseball coach at his alma mater.

5. CARL LEWIS

The Chicago Bulls drafted Lewis in the tenth round of the 1984 NBA draft. Overall, Lewis was the 212th pick of the draft. But the track star and nine-time gold medalist never considered a career in the NBA. His stature as an athlete was already secure after his incredible performance in the 1984 Olympic Games in Los Angeles, where he won four gold medals.

6. JORGE GONZALES

Gonzales is a legitimate 7′ 6″ and starred on the 1988 Argentina Olympic basketball team. He was drafted by the Atlanta Hawks but did not make it to the NBA. Instead, Gonzales turned to professional wrestling and started his career with World Championship Wrestling. He was billed as "El Gigante." Years later, Gonzales made the switch to the World Wrestling Federation, where he competed against the likes of the Undertaker, even eliminating the ghoulish 'Taker from the 1993 Royal Rumble match.

7. OSCAR SCHMIDT

Schmidt was a Brazilian superstar nicknamed "Mao Santa," or Holy Hand. Oscar was a deadly long range shooter, once scoring 46 points in a 1987 upset over the American team led by Danny Manning and David Robinson in the Pan-Am Games. The New Jersey Nets chose Schmidt with their sixth round pick in 1984 draft. Schmidt was satisfied to star in Brazil and Europe and was never tempted to try his luck in the NBA. The Brazilian scoring machine logged an unofficial count of 49,703 points, over 11,000 more than NBA scoring champion Kareem Abdul-Jabbar.

8. DENISE LONG

Long was the first woman ever drafted by the NBA. Taken in the 1969 draft by Franklin Mieuli, the owner of the San Francisco Warriors, the pick was void because in 1969 high school players were ineligible for the NBA draft. Denise had been a high school standout in Iowa's six-on-six girls basketball, scoring 111 points in one game and averaging 68.5 points per game in her senior year for Union-Whitten High School in Whitten, Iowa.

9. PETER GENT

A former Dallas Cowboy, Peter Gent inked the best-seller *North Dallas Forty* about life in professional football.

The movie was released in 1979 and the story was based on the early 1970s Dallas Cowboys. Gent was drafted in 1964 in the fourteen round by the Baltimore Bullets.

10. **BUBBA SMITH**

The former great defensive linemen with the Baltimore Colts—perhaps best known in some circles for his Miller Lite beer commercials—was drafted by the Baltimore Bullets in the eleventh round of the 1967 NBA draft. Smith later gained notoriety as a star in the *Policy Academy* movies.

When Basketball and Wrestling Collide

There have been several members of the NBA community who have ventured into the area of sports entertainment, drawing large pay-per-view crowds competing as professional wrestlers. But there have also been many pro wrestlers who had dreams of a career in the NBA before donning the tights. Here are ten such people:

1. **DENNIS RODMAN**

The rebounding machine known as "The Worm" has participated in four World Championship Wrestling pay-per view events, twice teaming with Hulk Hogan. Rodman made headlines for skipping out on obligations with the Chicago Bulls to participate in a televised wrestling show called "Nitro." Dennis was last seen in 2000, losing to the late Curt Henning via disqualification in a wrestling event held in Australia.

2. **KARL MALONE**

At a 1998 World Championship Wrestling tag-team extravaganza titled "Bash at the Beach," held in San

Diego, California, Utah Jazz forward Karl Malone teamed with Diamond Dallas Page against Hulk Hogan and Dennis "The Worm" Rodman.

3.   JEROME WILLIAMS

Toronto Raptors forward Williams, known as "The Junkyard Dog," has been a longtime professional wrestling fan. In his time away from the court, Williams has served limited roles in the wrestling arena as a professional wrestling manager, referee, and guest commissioner. On June 9, 2001, during a World Wrestling Entertainment Extravaganza held at the Air Canada Centre in Toronto, Canada, Williams was the special guest referee in a ladies tag-team bout featuring Trish Stratus and Jacqueline versus Lita and Molly Holly.

4.   DARRYL DAWKINS

Dawkins, or "Chocolate Thunder," was a judge in Wrestlemania 2 for a boxing match that took place on April 7, 1986, in Uniondale, N.Y., pitting "Rowdy" Roddy Piper against *Rocky III* villian, Mr. T. Mr. T won the slugfest when the match was prematurely stopped via disqualification, thus sparing Dawkins and the other celebrity judges—Cab Calloway and G. Gordon Liddy—from revealing their scores of the match.

5.   MARK CUBAN

Dallas Mavericks owner Mark Cuban was sitting ringside for the "Survivor Series," a pay-per-view professional wrestling event presented by the World Wrestling Entertainment at the American Airlines Center in Dallas, Texas in November 2003. Cuban, a confessed lifelong fan, became part of the show. Eric Bischoff, a member of the professional wrestling world, began to heckle Cuban who responded by jumping into the ring to the enjoyment of the capacity crowd. Randy Orton, a wrestler and friend to Bischoff, rushed to the ring and applied his patent move, "The RKO," to Cuban. Rumors of the Maverick's owner making a career in wrestling entertainment were soon squashed.

6. **PAUL WHITE**

Paul "The Giant" White—known in wrestling circles as "The Big Show"—went to Wichita State University on a basketball scholarship. In high school, Wight averaged 30 points per game for Wyman King Academy in Batesburg, South Carolina. At Wichita State, Wight averaged only 2 points per game. Using Hulk Hogan as a role model, Wight turned his aspirations toward professional wrestling, and eventually defeated Rick Flair for a world title in 1996.

7. **KEVIN NASH**

Nash played college basketball for the University of Tennessee in the late 1970s, scoring 5.1 points and 4 rebounds per game as a junior. The following year Nash was thrown off the team for violating team rules. Nash relocated to Europe where he played pro basketball for several years, but his career ended in 1985 after he tore an anterior cruciate ligament (ACL) playing in Germany. Nash tried out with the Cleveland Cavaliers but was soon waived, which eventually led him to the squared circle. Nash has been a prominent grappler in both World Championship Wrestling and the WWE, where he started out as a bodyguard named Diesel, and eventually worked his way up to "World Champion" status.

8. JONATHAN COLEMAN

The former leading scorer for the McPherson College Bulldogs played college ball in the mid-1990s. Coachman is now a professional wrestling announcer with Vince McMahon's World Wrestling Entertainment. "The Coach," as he is known in professional wrestling circles, has feuded with Jerry "The King" Lawler and "Stone Cold" Steve Austin. Coachman's most embarrassing moment occurred on March 30, 2003 when he was pinned at Wrestlemania 19 by a female grappler.

9. PAULO "GIANT" SILVA

Standing 7' 3", Silva is a former member of the 1992 Brazilian Olympic basketball team. Silva performed in the World Wrestling Federation in 1998 in the group known as "The Oddities." He later switched to competing in mixed martial arts matches, where the 400-pound big man has had mixed results.

10. LINDA MILES

Linda Miles is now known as "Shaniqua" in wrestling circles. Miles played four years of college basketball for Rutgers, averaging more than 7 points and 5 rebounds per game in her career. After an attempt at the WNBA, Miles turned to wrestling. She won the Tough Enough 2 competition for beginning wrestlers, and has parlayed that performance into a successful wrestling career.

Basketball Tragedies

Basketball stars are often thought of as invincible, infallible demigods. Anyone with that much talent must be perfect, right? Wrong. Below is a list of basketball tragedies that befell even the greatest of players.

1. EARVIN "MAGIC" JOHNSON AND HIV

Who can forget where they were on November 7, 1991, as Earvin "Magic" Johnson announced to the world that he was infected with the HIV virus? Johnson announced his immediate retirement, leaving the basketball world in shock. Many feared that a painful death loomed in Magic's near future, but the former Laker great has defied the odds and has been living a productive life since his diagnosis. Johnson has been inspiring many as well as educating millions of people on the subject of AIDS.

2. HANK GATHERS COLLAPSES ON THE COURT

Former NCAA scoring and rebounding champion Hank Gathers of Loyola Marymount University had been on medication for an irregular heartbeat during the final months of the 1989–90 season. In a postseason conference tournament game against Portland, Gathers jammed an impressive dunk early in the game and then retreated down the court. He soon slumped to the ground and went into a seizure. Gathers died several hours later.

3. THE FATEFUL PUNCH

On December 9, 1977, Los Angeles Lakers power forward Kermit Washington threw a haymaker punch during a basketball melee that landed flush on the face of the unsuspecting Houston Rocket, Rudy Tomjanovich. Lakers assistant coach Jack McCloskey said it was "the hardest punch in the history of mankind." Tomjanovich never saw the punch coming and almost died as a result of the injuries he sustained from it. Rudy had a fractured skull, jaw, and nose, and was leaking spinal fluid. Tomjanovich later made a full recovery after going through extensive reconstructive surgery.

4. LEN BIAS AND COCAINE

Len Bias was picked second overall in the 1986 NBA draft by the Boston Celtics. Boston fans were ecstatic to be adding the Maryland University star to an already legendary line-up that included Larry Bird, Robert Parish, and Kevin McHale. Many basketball experts predicted that Bias would be a future All-Star, but Bias would never suit up for the Celtics. He died from a cocaine overdose just forty-eight hours after the draft.

5. REGGIE LEWIS DIES WHILE SHOOTING HOOPS

Popular Boston Celtics player Reggie Lewis passed away on July 27, 1993, while shooting baskets in preparation for the upcoming season. Although it stunned the sports world, Lewis had been diagnosed with a heart condition after he collapsed on the court in a 1993 playoff game against the Charlotte Hornets. Several in the media and medical professions questioned Lewis's return to professional basketball, but Reggie planned to continue playing despite those concerns.

6. THE DEATH OF DRAZEN PETROVIC

Petrovic grew up in a small port city on the Adriatic Sea in Croatia, and learned to play basketball with his older brother. Petrovic played in his final game on June 6, 1993, against Slovenia in Wroclow, Poland. Drazen opted to drive home with a friend, and during a heavy storm near Denkendorf, Germany, the vehicle carrying him slammed into a truck. It killed the NBA player instantly.

7. MAURICE STOKES

Maurice Stokes was a top NBA forward in the 1950s who averaged more than 17 points per game. During a game in his third year in the league with the Cincinnati Royals, Stokes was fouled and lost his balance. He fell to the floor, was knocked unconscious, and a few days later Maurice went into a coma and was paralyzed. Teammate and friend Jack Twyman became his legal guardian and helped raise money to cover Stokes's medical expenses. A movie called *Maurice* aired three years after Stokes's death in 1970. "The first great, athletic power forward," was how former Celtics great and NBA coach Bob Cousy described Stokes. "He was Karl Malone with more finesse."

8. JABBAR DECKS BENSON

While most people know about the "The Punch" thrown by Kermit Washington at Rudy Tomjanovich, roughly forty other fights occurred during that 1977–78 NBA season. On opening night, October 18, 1977, at the Milwaukee Arena, Kareem Abdul-Jabbar leveled rookie and first draft pick Kent Benson. About four minutes into the game, Abdul-Jabbar and Benson traded elbows and pushed each other in the lane. Angered by Benson's elbows, Abdul-Jabbar blind sided him with a right hook that floored the rookie. Another Bucks rookie at the time, Ernie Grunfeld said, "It was not the way to start a career. It wasn't something you see every day." Benson never reached his full potential as a dominant force in the NBA, and many believe that he never mentally recovered from the punch he took from Kareem Abdul-Jabbar in his first professional basketball game.

q.   TRAGIC SUICIDE

Sacramento Kings shooting guard Ricky Berry took his own life after his rookie season on August 14, 1989. Barry had been the Kings first round draft pick the previous year, from San Jose State.

10.   LANDON TURNER

Landon Turner is the only paraplegic ever to be drafted in the history of the NBA. Turner played for Bob Knight and started on the Hoosiers' 1981 national championship team, led by Isiah Thomas. Four months following the NCAA championship victory , Turner was involved in an automobile accident that left the 6' 10" forward paralyzed from his chest down. The Boston Celtics picked Turner in the tenth round of the NBA draft. Today, Turner is a motivational speaker.

ABA Uniqueness

The American Basketball Association ended in 1976 after a wild, nine-year ride. The league produced stars like Julius "Dr. J" Erving, Moses Malone and David "The Skywalker" Thompson. The ABA's wild nature was immortalized in sportswriter Terry Pluto's book, *Loose Balls*. The league didn't have the financial power of the NBA, however, and it eventually folded. Several gimmicks used to attract fans were unique to the ABA, and even a few made it to the NBA. Below are several noteworthy spectacles put on by the ABA.

1. THE SLAM DUNK CONTEST

The original slam dunk contest came into existence in the final year of the ABA at the 1976 All-Star Game in Denver. The ABA team owners were concerned about attendance and hoped that adding the dunk contest as a gimmick would draw more fans to the All-Star Game. The participants were Larry Kenon, Artis Gilmore, David Thompson, George Gervin, and Julius Erving.

Sports Illustrated called it "the best halftime invention since the restroom." Dunks were judged based on creativity and fan response and Julius Erving was the contest's first winner.

2. THREE-POINT SHOT

The three-point shot was implemented to bring more excitement to the ABA for the fans. It also forced teams to think more about their outside game. ABA commissioner George Mikan compared the three-point shot to the home run in baseball. The ABA used the three-point shot from its inception, but had borrowed the idea from the defunct ABL.

3. THE BALL

The original red, white, and blue basketball got approval from the ABA's first commissioner, the legendary George Mikan. The reason for the unique ball was to give the upstart league an identity of its own, separate from the NBA. Mikan reasoned that, since the name of the league was the American Basketball Association, the colors, red, white and blue should be used to symbolize America's colors. Mikan also thought that the ball would be more visible for the fans and for television audiences.

4. NO FOUL OUTS

In the ABA's final season the "no foul-out rule" was implemented. Even after a player committed their sixth personal foul, he could remain in the game. However, ensuing fouls by the player with six or more fouls consequently gave two free throws and ball possession to the other team.

N.C. State Media Relations

David Thompson shows why he was selected
for the original slam-dunk contest.

5. THE HUMAN BILLBOARD

Minnesota Pipers star Connie Hawkins' 1968–69 warm-up suit was covered in advertisements, a large picture of the colorful league ball, and Hawkins' post-season awards from the previous year with the champion Pittsburgh Pipers. Since Hawkins was the lone Piper forced to wear the advertisements, he soon grew tired of the heckling and eventually "misplaced" the warm-up jacket while traveling to a road game.

6. FEMALE PLAYER

In 1968, jockey Penny Ann Early became the first female to participate in a professional men's basketball game when she suited up for the Kentucky Colonels. Early became a controversial figure in Kentucky when she became the first licensed female jockey in the country. The rest of the jockeys at Churchill Downs shunned Early and refused to enter any race she was in. In a media ploy, the Kentucky Colonels signed Early to a contract even though she wasn't much for basketball.

The Colonels' head coach, Gene Rhodes, was less than thrilled with his new player, but management won out and on November 28, 1968, Early played briefly in a game. Seconds after taking the court, Penny Ann passed the ball inbounds to teammate Bobby Rascoe, who called for a timeout. Early then exited the court to a loud ovation, never to be seen again in professional basketball.

7. ZIGGY THE DOG, OWNER

In the years of the ABA, many basketball fans thought Joe and Mamie Gregory were the owners of the Kentucky

Colonels. However, the true owner was arguably the Gregory's dog, Ziggy. Ziggy attended the ABA owners' meetings, had his own seat for home games, and flew first-class to road games. Season ticket holders who purchased "The Ziggy Package" received admittance to the Ziggy Room hospitality suite. Ziggy—whose full name was Champion Gaystock Le Monsignor—was a Brussels Griffon show dog that won more than 100 championships, and had almost forty different uniforms to wear at Colonels home games.

8. INTIMIDATION NIGHT

Before the 1971–72 season, Pittsburgh Condors star John Brisker vowed to lead the league in scoring, or knock out all adversaries who defended him if he didn't win the scoring title. During an early season game in Pittsburgh, Brisker was held to only 4 points at halftime by the Utah Stars. Brisker's temper soon ignited and he rumbled with several Stars' players. On November 4, 1971, Pittsburgh played in Salt Lake City, and the Stars' promotional executives titled the evening, "John Brisker Intimidation Night." The game's program read:

> Tonight it is Brisker who is on foreign soil and with the likes of Ron Lyle, Bill Daniels' professional boxer from Denver, Don and Gene Fullmer, Rex Layne, and Tony Doyle standing in the wing, best he doesn't get far out of line.

9. THE WRESTLING BEAR

Throughout the years, the Indiana Pacers hosted a few unique halftime events. In April 1975, the Pacers halftime show featured an act with a live grizzly bear named Victor. The evening's promotional program read: "Victor will be at the game to take on such noted wrestlers as Chet Coppock, sports director at WISH-TV, Reb Porter at WIFE radio, and several other special opponents. If time permits, Victor will also wrestle a couple of fans."

10. BOB "SLICK" LEONARD NIGHT

Bob "Slick" Leonard won more games than any coach in ABA history, including three championships with the Indiana Pacers. His teams never missed the playoffs. During the 1972–73 season, the Pacers were playing the Utah Stars on the road when a controversy erupted. Utah won the game, but Slick thought the shot clock had gone off before Utah scored a key basket near the end of the contest. Leonard was ejected and given two technical fouls. In a fit of rage, Leonard ran back on the court, grabbed the ball, and kicked it into the crowd.

Showing a good sense of humor, Stars management turned the outburst into a promotional event for the Pacers' next visit to town. Leonard's mug was featured on the front of the official Utah-Indiana program, and before the opening tip-off, Leonard was presented with a framed picture of the incident. The good-natured Leonard took it all in stride.

Enforcers

Not all players can be graceful scorers. Some are best known for their ability to physically intimidate their opponents. The following is a list of ten players of all sizes and positions who threw their weight around in pro basketball.

1. RICK MAHORN

Rick Mahorn used his wide posterior and bulk to intimidate nearly everyone he played. He teamed with widebody Jeff Ruland for the Washington Bullets to form the duo that famed Celtics announcer Johnny Most called "McFilthy and McNasty." Mahorn engaged in some nasty battles in his years with the Bullets, the Philadephia 76ers, and the Detroit Pistons. Mahorn was considered to be the baddest of the Pistons' legendary "Bad Boys" squad that captured back-to-back NBA titles in 1989 and 1990.

2. CHARLES OAKLEY

Charles Oakley used his physical strength to become one of the game's best rebounders. His first few years in the league he played with the Chicago Bulls, and one of his main jobs was to protect the team's prized player, Michael Jordan. Later, Oakley was traded to the New York Knicks and teamed with center Patrick Ewing to form an imposing front line. Oakley was never afraid of physical confrontations, even during warm-ups. He even slapped opposing players Jeff McInnis and Tyrone Hill before games began.

3. MAURICE LUCAS

Maurice Lucas earned his keep as one of the original enforcers of the NBA during the 1970s. In fact, his nickname was "The Enforcer." Like many NBA greats, he began his career in the more flamboyant ABA, playing for the St. Louis Spirits and the Kentucky Colonels. While he was with the Spirits, Lucas decked behemoth center Artis Gilmore. In the NBA, Lucas played a huge role in leading the Portland Trail Blazers to the 1977 NBA title, as he teamed with center Bill Walton to form one of the best front courts in the league.

4. XAVIER MCDANIEL

Known as the "X-Man," McDaniel was a rugged 6' 7" 210-pound small forward who played anything but little. One of the most frightening photos in NBA history shows McDaniel with a choke hold on small guard Wes Matthews. The *1988 Complete Handbook of Pro Basketball* described McDaniel aptly: "In just two years in the NBA, he's fought with just about everybody except the mayor of Seattle."

5. KERMIT WASHINGTON

Kermit Washington was a tough power forward who is often unfortunately remembered for one fateful punch.

On December 9, 1977, Washington began tussling with the Rockets' Kevin Kunnert, when Rocket teammate Rudy Tomjonavich came rushing to help break up the fight. Washington, who thought he was being attacked, turned around and landed what has become known as "The Punch." Bestselling sportswriter John Feinstein even wrote a book about Washington and Tomjonavich called *The Punch*.

6. WARREN JABALI

Warren Armstrong changed his name to Warren Jabali in 1969. Though he stood only 6′ 2″, he was arguably the most feared player in the history of the ABA. League officials suspended Jabali for fifteen days after stomping Jim Jarvis in the face. Dan Issel spoke of Jabali in Terry Pluto's *Loose Balls*: "I played with Jabali later in his career in Kentucky and our whole team was scared to death of the guy because he was so mean."

7. JOHN BRISKER

John Brisker was a 6′ 5″ forward who terrified opposing players and teammates alike. ABA star Mack Calvin said in Pluto's *Loose Balls*: "John Brisker scared everybody. Even the guys on his own team were frightened of the guy." For his two and a half years in the ABA, Brisker was also a great scorer, averaging 26 points per game. After his playing days were over, Brisker allegedly served as a mercenary soldier in Africa. One rumor holds that he was killed in Uganda. In a July 2004 piece for the *Seattle Post-Intelligencer*, Robert Jamieson wrote about the various wild rumors associated with Brisker's demise in Africa. He concludes: "All anyone knows is the ungentle giant shone briefly for the Supersonics and veered out of sight."

8. CALVIN MURPHY

A 5' 9" scoring guard and thirteen-year NBA veteran, Murphy may have been the smallest enforcer in the league. Calvin had boxed as a teenager in Connecticut and claimed to be 17–0 in his fights. Being smaller than most other basketball players and excelling at baton twirling as a youth gave Calvin reasons to learn self-defense. Among some of Murphy's rivals were Norm Van Lier, Norm Nixon, and 6' 8", 225-pound forward Sidney Wicks. Wicks once started a fight that Calvin amazingly finished by jumping up and grabbing the taller player by his hair, pulling him down to closer to eye level, and raining punches on him.

9. "JUNGLE JIM" LOSCUTOFF

This Boston Celtic enforcer arrived in Beantown in the mid-1950s to toughen up the Celtics squad. Loscutoff helped Bill Russell's Celtics by punishing rival centers. "Jungle Jim" had a limited offensive arsenal, scoring ten or more points only once during his nine years in Boston, but the bruising forward assisted his team to seven championships.

10. WENDELL LADNER

This former ABA enforcer rivaled John Brisker as the toughest man in the ABA. Known for his physical play, the farm-raised Ladner also had a temper that few dared to challenge. Wendell protected both Dan Issel of the Kentucky Colonels and Julius Erving of the New York Nets. During the 1971–72 season, Wendell was ejected from a game for "a malicious foul" on Rick Barry. Said Ladner following the game, "I sure wouldn't want to break his leg and put him up in bed with his family." Ladner also threw his shoe at Freddie Lewis during a playoff game.

Sexual Misconduct

I n 2003, the sporting world and the rest of the country
was rocked by news that Los Angeles Lakers superstar Kobe Bryant had been charged with the rape of
a young Colorado woman. All criminal charges were
dropped against Bryant in 2004. Of course, all criminal
defendants are entitled to the presumption of innocence in our judicial system, and just because someone is charged by prosecutors does not mean they are
guilty of the crime. On the other hand, some believe
there is a disturbing amount of crime committed by
NBA players. Investigative journalist and author Jeff
Benedict wrote *Out of Bounds: Inside the NBA's Culture of Rape, Violence and Crime*, dealing specifically
with the subject. The following ten basketball players
faced charges for sexual crimes.

1. KOBE BRYANT

Los Angeles Lakers superstar Kobe Bryant was
charged with raping a nineteen-year-old Colorado
woman, an employee at a Boulder spa resort. Bryant
contended that it was simply a matter of consensual

sex. The case promised to be one of the nation's highest profile trials, but all charges were eventually dropped, and Bryant apologized to the woman for his actions on that night. The alleged victim filed a civil suit against Bryant, which was settled. The terms were kept confidential.

2. TOM PAYNE

Tom Payne had a bright future as the first African-American player at the University of Kentucky. He played one year for the Atlanta Hawks, and at 7′ 2″ and 240 pounds, Payne could be a dominating presence. His former Atlanta Hawks coach Richie Guerin told Cox News Service: "He had the potential to be an outstanding center in the league for a dozen years, and maybe eventually a great one." However, Payne was hit with multiple convictions for rape. He is not scheduled for release from prison until he is sixty-five.

3. RUBEN PATTERSON

Ruben Patterson of the Portland Trailblazers is the NBA's first registered sex offender. He allegedly forced his nanny to perform oral sex on him. He registered as a sex offender and was sentenced to fifteen days in jail. Patterson made a so-called "Alford plea" which means that a defendant can deny guilt while admitting that there are sufficient facts for a jury conviction.

4. ANTHONY MASON

Anthony Mason, a longtime NBA player, was arrested in 1998 on two counts of third-degree rape of two teenage girls. Mason pleaded guilty to the lesser charge of endangering the welfare of a child. He was sentenced to several years probation and 200 hours of community service.

5. JACK GIVENS

In June 2004, former Kentucky basketball great and former NBA player Jack Givens was arrested for sexual battery and molestation charges. Law enforcement officials claimed Givens inappropriately touched a fourteen-year-old girl. Givens, who works as a television color analyst for the Orlando Magic, vigorously denies the allegations.

6. CALVIN MURPHY

Former Houston Rockets great Calvin Murphy was charged in March 2004 with several counts of aggravated sexual assault of a child, for incidents that allegedly occurred from 1988 to 1991. The alleged victims were five children of Murphy's. Murphy vigorously maintained his innocence, and claimed the charges are part of a plan to extort money from him. In December 2004, a jury acquitted Murphy of the charges.

7. DESHAWN STEVENSON

In 2002, then–Utah Jazz player Deshawn Stevenson pleaded no contest to charges that he had sex with a fourteen-year-old girl. The girl told police that she willingly had sex with the 20-year-old Stevenson. He was sentenced to two years probation, and now plays for the Orlando Magic.

8. KEN WILBURN

Ken Wilburn, who played in the NBA and ABA from 1967 to 1969, was sentenced to eight years in prison for inappropriately touching two female minors. He was originally charged with counts of aggravated sexual assault.

9.   MARCUS WEBB

Marcus Webb, who played for the Boston Celtics during the 1992–93 season, was charged with raping a former girlfriend. He pleaded guilty to the lesser charge of indecent assault and was sentenced to thirty days in jail.

10.   ROHAN RUSSELL

Rohan Russell, who averaged 27 points per game for the Division III school Johnson & Wales, was convicted of two counts of first-degree sexual assault against a seventeen-year-old girl in April 2004.

They Played in One Pro Game

Professional b-ballers seek playing time, the life-blood of a basketball athlete. The following ten players appeared in a grand total of one professional basketball game, according to the "Player Registry" of *Total Basketball: the Ultimate Basketball Encyclopedia*. They exemplify the term benchwarmer.

1. RYAN ROBERTSON

Ryan Robertson probably set an NBA record for the most playing time for a player in only one NBA game. In the 1999–2000 season, Robertson played a total of twenty-five minutes for the Sacramento Kings. He collected 5 points during his time on the court.

2. BILL STRICKER

Bill Stricker, who played college basketball at Pacific, played one game for the Portland Trailblazers during the 1970–71 season. In two minutes of action Stricker scored 4 points.

3. LARRY CONLEY

Larry Conley, who played college basketball for the University of Kentucky, played one game for the ABA's Kentucky Colonels during the 1967–68 season. He logged eighteen minutes on the court, collecting a mere 2 points.

4. MARK BAKER

Mark Baker, who played college ball at Ohio State, played one game for the Toronto Raptors during the 1998–99 season. He played two minutes, which left him enough time to commit 1 turnover.

5. RON DORSEY

Ron Dorsey, who played college ball at Tennessee State, played one game for the Carolina Cougars in the ABA. He played twelve minutes, scored 4 points, and grabbed 5 rebounds.

6. BLAINE DENNING

Blaine Denning, who played college ball at Lawrence Tech, played one game for the Baltimore Bullets of the NBA during the 1952–53 season. He played for nine minutes, with 5 points and 4 rebounds.

7. JARRETT DURHAM

Jarrett Durham, who played college basketball at Duquesne, played in one game for the New York Nets of the ABA in the 1971–72 season. He did not collect a single point or rebound for his efforts.

8. BARRY SUMPTER

Barry Sumpter, a 6′ 11″ center from Austin Peay, played one game for the Los Angeles Clippers during the 1988–89 season. He played less than one minute and did not score a single point or grab a rebound.

9. **RATKO VARDA**

Bosnia's Ratko Varda played one game for the Boston Celtics in the 2002–03 season. He scored 5 points, grabbed 3 rebounds, and committed 3 personal fouls in six minutes of action.

10. **LARRY SYKES**

Larry Sykes, who played college ball at Xavier, played in one game for the Boston Celtics during the 1995–96 season. He played for two minutes and collected 2 points.

Playground Legends

Many basketball players achieved greatness in their own unique way with the improvisional nature of streetball. Not every player can thrive in a team-oriented environment with rigid disciplinary controls imposed by a coach. Some individuals simply were at their best playing playground basketball in Rucker Park or other such places. Currently, playground basketball has made a major comeback with the Entertainer's Basketball Classic (EBC) at Rucker Park and the Street Ball Association. The following ten individuals were among the greatest playground legends.

1. EARL MANIGAULT

Many consider the greatest streetballer of all-time to be Earl "The Goat" Manigault. None other than Kareem Abdul-Jabbar called Manigault the greatest basketball player he ever faced on a court. He allegedly possessed a 50-inch vertical leap that enabled him to rise over much taller defenders. Manigault is also allegedly the originator of the "Double Dunk": a move where a player dunks the ball with one hand, catches it with the other hand, and then dunks again. Kicked out of Benjamin Franklin High School his senior year, Manigault enrolled at Johnson C. Smith University where he lasted less than a year. He served a prison term for possession of drugs and later failed an ABA tryout in 1970. Fortunately, Manigault eventually conquered drugs and ran a basketball program for inner-city youth. His life was captured in the HBO film *Rebound*. Manigault died in 1998 of congestive heart failure at the age of 53.

2. **JOE HAMMOND**

Joe "The Destroyer" Hammond is considered by many to be the greatest offensive force among playground legends. He never played high school or college basketball, but he routinely lit up NBA stars on the playground. Vincent M. Mallozzi, in his book *Asphalt Gods: An Oral History of the Rucker Tournament*, tells the story of how Hammond was offered a tryout and practiced with the Los Angeles Lakers. Hammond made at least 18 shots in a row in a scrimmage with the Lakers, and allegedly turned down a $50,000 contract, saying he could make more money in the street.

3. **"PEE WEE" KIRKLAND**

Richard "Pee Wee" Kirkland was a playground legend who led the Rucker League in scoring for three consecutive years in the early 1970s. Mallozzi quotes former NBA great Nate "Tiny" Archibald on Kirkland: "While I think Joe Hammond was maybe the best offensive player to come off the playgrounds, I seriously believe that Pee Wee Kirkland was the best all-around player." Kirkland averaged more than 40 points per game at Kittrell Junior College in North Carolina, and later played for Norfolk State in Virginia. Drafted by the Chicago Bulls in 1968, Kirkland quit the Bulls to return to a street life. He eventually turned his life around and ran a basketball school for kids, and played a bit part in the 1994 movie *Above the Rim*.

4. JACKIE JACKSON

"Jumping" Jackie Jackson was a true playground legend who earned immortality with his moves against the great Wilt Chamberlain in a 1962 street game. Chamberlain, the most dominant player in NBA history, turned to the basket for a shot, and the 6' 5" Jackson came out of nowhere to block it. Kareem Abdul-Jabbar wrote of the play in his autobiography *Giant Steps*: "It was the most amazing play I've ever seen on the court, and the whole place went crazy." Jackson played at Virginia Union and for a time with the Harlem Globetrotters.

5. RAFER ALSTON

Rafer Alston is a point guard for the Toronto Raptors, and has also played for the Milwaukee Bucks and the Miami Heat. However, Alston made his name on the playgrounds as "Skip to My Lou," for his ability to dribble past defenders as easy as "one, two, skip to my Lou." Alston is a master at the look-away pass, crossover dribble, and spin moves. Jerry Tarkanian recruited Alston in New York to come play for Fresno State, though Alston first played for two years at a community college in Fresno.

6. JAMES "FLY" WILLIAMS

James "Fly" Williams honed his game on the playgrounds of Brownsville, New York, where he was born. Immortalized in Rick Telander's 1976 book *Heaven Is a*

Austin Peay University

James "Fly" Williams.

Playground, Williams scored on the playground, set an NCAA scoring record for freshman at Austin Peay State University that stood for more than fifteen years, and even played one year in the ABA. He scored 63 points on Moses Malone in the Dapper Dan Tournament, a high school All-Star game. But Fly was at his best on the playground where his improvisional genius could blossom. Telander wrote: "In the game, Fly, who got his name on the Brooklyn playgrounds because he let 'fly' the ball, started shooting almost before he came across midcourt. He waved his arms, he pointed at opponents, he showed a contortionist's range of expression. Sometimes he left defenders so entangled in their own legs he laughed at them as he drove past."

7. LLOYD DANIELS

Lloyd "Swee'pea" Daniels was a 6′ 8″ guard who could do it all, though he nearly threw it all away. John Valenti quoted Nate "Tiny" Archibald in his book *Swee'Pea and Other Playground Legends*: "He's the best. As far as entertainment, he's gonna do some shit you've never seen before." A high school All-American, Daniels averaged a triple double his junior year in high school—31 points, 12 rebounds and 10 assists per game. As a twenty-year-old rookie in the CBA, Daniels averaged better than 16 points and nearly 5 assists per game. However, Daniels's life was beset by problems. He was shot in a drug deal gone wrong and never made it into UNLV, despite being heavily recruited by Jerry Tarkanian. It looked like Daniels would never escape his personal demons. But in 1992, Tarkanian became coach of the San Antonio Spurs and he gave Daniels— already past his prime—a shot in the NBA. Daniels averaged 9 points per game for the Spurs. He bounced around the NBA, played overseas, and even played in the IBL in Las Vegas for a time. Though he escaped his demons, many wonder how good Daniels would have been if he had avoided trouble in his prime.

8. BILLY REISER

Earl "The Pearl" Monroe was known as "Black Jesus" for the incredible spin moves he showcased on New York playgrounds. Monroe, of course, went on to a Hall of Fame-caliber career in the NBA. Billy Reiser was another basketball playground legend with a similar nickname—"White Jesus." Reiser was a 6' 4" player from East Harlem who possessed a 44-inch vertical leap. Mallozzi writes in *Asphalt Gods*: "Like Earl Monroe before him, Reiser's nickname was a tribute to his miraculous game." Reiser played college basketball at Centenary and Eastern Kentucky, but injuries deprived him of a professional career.

9. HERMAN KNOWINGS

Nicknamed "The Helicopter," Herman Knowings was born in South Carolina but moved to Harlem as a youngster. He was known for his incredible hangtime and ability to block the shots of players much taller than his 6' 5" frame. Mallozzi quotes a former New York City playground player on Knowings, "I miss the Copter. We all do man. That guy, I swear, he used to fly like an angel." According to John Valenti, Knowings died in April 1980 when his cab was struck by another vehicle.

10. LARRY WILLIAMS

Larry Williams is known as the "Bone Collector" for his knack for leaving people in the dust on the basketball court with knee-twisting, ankle-breaking moves. In 2001, Williams won the MVP of the Entertainer's Basketball Classic, held at the legendary Rucker Park. He is a lead attraction in the Street Ball Association.

Pro Basketball Mascots

Professional basketball is not only a sport but also high-dollar entertainment. With ticket prices that are far from cheap, fans deserve to be entertained. The following mascots do their best to ensure that levity has its rightful place in NBA arenas.

1. THE GORILLA

The Gorilla has been thrilling basketball fans for the Phoenix Suns since 1980. The dynamic dunking Gorilla has been a longtime NBA favorite and is also an asset to the community of Phoenix. The Gorilla often visits schools and charities, and has even started his own reading incentive program in Phoenix called "Book the Gorilla," where he challenges children to write stories.

2. LUCKY THE LEPRECHAUN

The Boston Celtics fan favorite, Lucky the Leprechaun, has more energy than most fabled little men. The crowd-friendly Lucky has been a part of Celtic history for all sixteen championship years. Lucky the Leprechaun

signs all his autographs with the number seventeen—
hoping to add another NBA title to the Celtics' history.

3. BANGO

The Milwaukee Bucks popular former announcer Eddie
Doucette used to shout "Bango" whenever a Milwaukee Buck scored on a long-range shot. Bango the Buck
came into being on October 18, 1977, when the Bucks
faced a home season-opener against the Los Angeles
Lakers and former Bucks star Kareem Abdul-Jabbar.
The Bucks had held a contest prior to the season
opener to name the Bucks' mascot.

4. MOONDOG

The city of Cleveland boasts the Rock-n-Roll Hall of
Fame, and is known for its musical past. Legendary
Cleveland radio disc-jockey, Alan Freed, coined the
phrase "Rock and Roll," and started a music explosion.
Freed was known as "Moondog" and his listeners were
called "moondoggers." The Cleveland Cavaliers adopted
Moondog as their mascot in honor of Freed.

5. HUGO THE HORNET

This mascot came to life in Charlotte on November 4,
1988. Since then, Hugo has entertained fans with his
acrobatics and hilarious routines. At times the hornet
will transform into his alter-ego, "Super Hugo," and
stun crowds with flashy dunks. These include the "Flip
Dunk," "Helmet Dunk," and the popular "Bug on the
Windshield Dunk." Hugo is a three-time NBA Mascot
Slam Dunk Champion. In recent years, Hugo has developed a third identity known as "Air Hugo," which is
an inflated version of the Hornets mascot.

6. **GRIZZ**

The fun-loving mascot of the Memphis Grizzlies, Grizz is an added attraction at Grizzlies home games. Either on the court or in the stands, Grizz can be spotted mingling with fans and amusing the crowd with his side-splitting antics. At halftime, Grizz goes to his den at The Pyramid and returns as a new character, "Super Grizz." Super Grizz wears a cape, mask, and chest shield, and gets the crowd fired up for the final two quarters using his high-flying acrobatics and mystifying dunks.

7. **BURNIE**

The popular Heat mascot has pulled numerous pranks in his fourteen years in the league, including a silly-string brawl with Bill Cosby, singing on stage with Jimmy Buffett, sitting on Jack Nicholson's lap, and flicking Bill Murray's ear. Burnie even smooched Sharon Stone, boogied with Madonna, threw to Cal Ripken Jr., and sparred with the cinematic Rocky Balboa himself, Sylvester Stallone, at mid-court.

8. **CRUNCH**

Crunch of the Minnesota Timberwolves has developed a standing as one of the most entertaining mascots in the league since his debut in 1989. He has performed frequently at NBA All-Star Weekends, and has also performed internationally in England and Australia.

9. **STUFF**

Stuff the Magic Dragon of the Orlando Magic is a big-bellied, friendly dragon who sports a pink and blue Mohawk and has radioactive green fur. Some of Stuff's tricks are sledding the stairs, swiping a fan's popcorn, shooting trick shots, dunking donuts, joking with NBA referees, teasing opposing teams' fans, and flirting with the ladies.

10. SQUATCH

This tall furry mascot of the Seattle Supersonics is a distant relative of the Yeti. Squatch supposedly grew tired of the mountain life and ventured to Seattle to look for work, including a brief movie career as a stunt double for Harry in *Harry and the Hendersons*. Squatch can now be seen dunking balls at every Sonics home game, and other stunts too risky for slighter primates.

Cameron Crazies

D uke University is known for its great basketball program under Coach Mike Krzyzewski. Duke has an incredible homecourt advantage at Cameron Indoor Stadium, as well. The students are seated in the first few rows, right on the court, unlike at many other colleges and universities. The students are known for their intensity and often ingenious cheers and jeers directed at opposing players. The following are ten of the most memorable antics of the Duke fans, appropriately dubbed "Cameron Crazies."

1. HERMAN VEAL

Herman Veal was a rugged Maryland forward known for his tough interior play and musclebound physique. In 1983, Veal was accused of sexually assaulting a female student. On his next trip to Cameron, the Duke crowd showered Veal with hundreds of panties. Additionally, Duke fans often throw tennis balls across the court before gametime. When Veal was announced, the Cameron Crazies threw tennis balls wrapped in condoms.

2. STEVE HALE

Steve Hale was a talented guard for the University of North Carolina—Duke's hated rival. Hale had suffered a collapsed lung prior to a game. In 1986, when Hale and the Tar Heels came to Duke, some of the Cameron Crazies gave their own medical advice: "In-Hale, Ex-Hale, In-Hale, Ex-Hale."

3. NIGEL DIXON

Nigel "Big Jelly" Dixon was a large center who tipped the scales at 6′ 11″ and 350 pounds for the Florida State Seminoles (he later transferred to Western Kentucky). Duke's starting center was the slender Casey Sanders. The Cameron Crazies came up with their own unique chant, looking first at Sanders and then at Dixon. The chant was: "Casey Sanders, Colonel Sanders."

4. DENNIS SCOTT

Dennis Scott was a deadly shooter and remarkable offensive talent for the Georgia Tech Yellow Jackets. However, Scott also battled the bulge during his college career. When he came to Cameron, Duke fans bombarded him with Twinkies.

5. CHRIS WASHBURN

North Carolina State's talented but troubled center, Chris Washburn, was accused of stealing a stereo. When he made his visit to Cameron, the faithful Duke fans showered Washburn with headphones, album covers, and albums. The crowd also gave their own Biblical chant: "Thou shalt not steal."

6. DETLEF SCHREMPF

Detlef Schrempf was a star forward for the University of Washington Huskies. From Germany, Schrempf was known for his long routine at the foul line. The Cameron Crazies would chant "Fehlwurf! Fehlwurf!"—German for "airball"—when he stepped to the free throw line, and counted aloud his number of dribbles.

7. TOM BURLESON

Tom Burleson, North Carolina State's star center in the early 1970s, was accused of breaking a pinball machine in college. When he came to Cameron, the Duke band played The Who's "Pinball Wizard."

8. MOE RIVERS

North Carolina State guard Moe Rivers had allegedly stolen aspirin in 1974. When Rivers came to Cameron, Duke fans tried to give him a headache by throwing aspirin tablets at him. *Sports Illustrated*'s Seth Davis referred to this in a 2001 article as the Crazies' "Best Pharmaceutical Display."

9. OLDEN POLYNICE

Before his long NBA career, Olden Polynice followed the great Ralph Sampson as the University of Virginia's starting center. Polynice encountered academic difficulties at Virginia in the form of plagiarism charges. When Polynice visited Cameron, the Duke faithful broke into the following chant: "Where's Olden?—At the copy machine."

10. DAVID ROBINSON

David Robinson helped the Navy Midshipmen to unprecedented heights as he grew from 6′ 6″ to a 7′ 1″ offensive force. Navy was hopelessly behind in one game against the Blue Devils, and the Duke fans chanted: "Abandon Ship, Abandon Ship!"

Bibliography

Abdul-Jabbar, Kareem and Peter Knobler. *Giant Steps*. New York: Bantam Books, 1983.

Benedict, Jeff. *Out of Bounds: Inside the NBA's Culture of Rape, Violence, & Crime*. New York: Harper-Collins, 2004.

Bjarkman, Peter C. *The Biographical History of Basketball*. Lincolnwood, Illinois: Masters Press, 2000.

Bogues, Tyrone & David Levine. *In the Land of the Giants*. Boston: Little, Brown and Company, 1994.

Hollander, Zander (ed.) *The Complete Handbook of Pro Basketball*. New York: Signet Books, 1974–1990. (annual publication)

Issel, Dan and Buddy Martin. *Parting Shots*. Chicago: Contemporary Books, Inc., 1986.

Johnson, Gary K., *Official 2004 Final Four Tournament Records*. Indianapolis: The National Collegiate Athletic Association, January 2004.

Johnson, Gary K. and Sean W. Straziscar. *Official 2004 NCAA Basketball Records*. Indianapolis: The National Collegiate Athletic Association, October 2003.

Keteyian, Armen, Harvey Araton and Martin F. Dardis. *Money Players: Days and Nights Inside the New NBA.* New York: Pocket Books, 1997.

Mallozzi, Vincent M. *Asphalt Gods: An Oral History of the Rucker Tournament.* New York: Doubleday, 2003.

Platt, Larry. *Only the Strong Survive: The Odyssey of Allen Iverson.* New York: ReganBooks, 2002.

Pluto, Terry. *Loose Balls.* New York: Fireside, 1990.

Postman, Andrew and Larry Stone. *The Ultimate Book of Sports Lists.* New York: Black Dog & Leventhal, 2003.

Shoulder, Ken, Bob Ryan, Sam Smith, Leonard Koppett and Bob Bellotti. *Total Basketball: The Ultimate Basketball Encyclopedia.* Wilmington, DE: SPORT Media Publishing, Inc., 2003.

Smallwood, John N. Jr. *Allen Iverson: Fear No One.* New York: Pocket Books, 2001.

Smith, Ron and John Gardella (eds.) *Official NBA Register: 2003–04 Edition.* St. Louis, Mo.: Sporting News, 2003.

Strasen, Marty. *The Best Book of Basketball Facts and Stats.* Buffalo: Firefly Books, 2003.

Valenti, John with Ron Naclerio. *Swee'Pea and Other Playground Legends: Tales of Drugs Violence and Basketball.* New York: Michael Kesend Publishing, Ltd., 1990.

Telander, Rick. *Heaven Is a Playground.* New York: Fireside (1988).

Index

Boldfaced page numbers refer to list entries.

About the Author

David L. Hudson, Jr. is the coauthor of *Boxing's Most Wanted™: The Top 10 Book of Champs, Chumps, and Punch-Drunk Palookas* (Potomac Books, Inc., 2004). An author, attorney, and lifelong basketball fan, he has written articles on basketball for both the Internet and print media and reviews sports books for the *Nashville Tennessean*. This is his tenth book. He lives near Nashville.